Christmas
in Illinois

May Theilgaard Watts

Christmas
in Illinois

EDITED BY James Ballowe

UNIVERSITY OF ILLINOIS PRESS

URBANA, CHICAGO, AND SPRINGFIELD

Frontispiece: Christmas tree, by May Theilgaard Watts

Library of Congress Cataloging-in-Publication Data
Christmas in Illinois / edited by James Ballowe.
p. cm.
ISBN 978-0-252-03442-8 (cloth : alk. Paper)
1. Christmas—Illinois.
2. Illinois—Social life and customs.
I. Ballowe, James.
GT4986.I3C57   2010
394.266309773—dc22   2010024452

In memory of my mother

Contents

Living Traditions

Songs and Symbols

Christmas Outdoors

Eating Merrily

Illustrations

Acknowledgments

This anthology results from the work of hundreds of people I have communicated with about Christmas. Many have composed pieces, edited pieces they have previously published, or helped me find stories and images from the past. Those whose names it is impossible to mention here are staff and volunteers at libraries, museums, genealogical societies, newspapers, and other institutions that serve the people of Illinois on a daily basis. These human and archival resources are as diverse as the State itself. For example, I am indebted to Preston Ewing, a citizen of Cairo, Illinois, who for years has volunteered to help preserve the rich history of that community at the confluence of the Mississippi and Ohio Rivers. I am no less indebted to Morag Walsh, Senior Archival Specialist in the Special Collections and Preservation Division of the Chicago Public Library, Harold Washington Center. Like their counterparts, these two, from far reaches of the state and with vastly different access to resources, devote their lives to preservation of the culture of Illinois.

I am equally indebted to those who provided their own images or helped me find historical images. Again, the contributions come from across the State. Art Geisert, formerly of Galena and now living in Bernard, Iowa, is a prolific creator of children's books, narrative etchings often based on a single-word title, as with his latest book, *Hogwash*. Charles Hammond, a resident of far southeastern Eldorado (originally Elder-Reado), Illinois, photographs scenes and restores images of deep Southern Illinois.

I am also indebted to the staff of the University of Illinois Press, who are passionate about making a book a pleasurable object to read and to hold.

Introduction

SEARCHING FOR CHRISTMAS IN ILLINOIS

In 1870, Ulysses S. Grant, the president of the United States with deep roots in Galena, Illinois, put his signature on a resolution that made December 25 a federal holiday. This meant that federal services would be halted on that day, and federal employees would have the day off. As with other federal holidays, the closing of the federal government reverberated throughout state and private sectors of the country. By the twentieth century, December 25 was considered by most Americans a holiday for all citizens.

For our Puritan colonial forefathers, declaring Christmas a national holiday would have been unthinkable. The Puritans, following the lead of their Commonwealth brethren in England, attempted to cleanse their communities of all manner of activity that they believed to be tainted by pagan, Anglican, or, especially, Roman mores. Thus, Christmas was banned during the early decades of the colonies and eschewed by many Protestant sects even until after the American Revolution.

Why? As the historians Stephen Nissenbaum in *The Battle for Christmas* and Bruce David Forbes in *Christmas: A Candid History* have pointed out, it was not just a rebellion against English culture and the Church of England that caused most early colonists to suppress Christmas observances. First, they knew that the date set for Christmas by the Catholic church—December 25—was an attempt to upstage celebrations of the winter solstice. Unlike Independence Day, which commemorates a date-certain event, Christmas Day was a holiday that few, especially Protestant Christians, could agree upon. More important perhaps was that the Christmas holiday celebrations that began in the fourth century A.D. and incorporated many pagan rituals and trappings had by the fifteenth century degenerated into misrule, if not into a pattern of social upheaval in which both the lower and upper classes often contrived to play a part. In many European communities on Christmas there was social inversion, a changing of places between the rich and the poor. Whenever those of wealth and power refused to play their part, the poor could make life difficult for them. Instead of agreed-upon pleasantries, the thwarted poor would perform annoying and sometimes destructive tricks on their would-be hosts. Christmas took on aspects of Halloween, including mummery and uncontrolled revelry. It was this sort of Christmas the Puritans most wanted to eliminate, along with the trappings that accompanied iconic Christmases associated with the Church of Rome.

The Illinois of Lincoln and Grant was well over a century removed from the repressive spirit of the Puritans. What had come between was eighteenth-century Deism and dependence upon reason and human sufficiency of the Founding Fathers; the Revolution that created a nation motivated by exploration and expansion; industrialization that accelerated immigration from Catholic Europe; the statehood of Illinois in 1818; and not least, the Victorian era, which spanned most of the nineteenth century and whose cultural influence pervaded America well into the twentieth.

Queen Victoria, with almost as much German blood as her Prince Consort, Albert of Saxony, was mother to nine children and grandmother to forty-two. While she was an empire builder and presided over the industrial and political evolution of her own country, she became a symbol in England and the United States for the virtues of domesticity and middle-class morality. To a great extent, she influenced the way we celebrate Christmas today in Illinois and the United States. During her lifetime, particularly after the Civil War, Christmas became the principal time of the year that domestic harmony prevailed and children were cynosures of doting adults.

Coincident with Victoria's iconic influence, the Christmas stories of Washington Irving, Charles Clement Moore's "A Visit from St. Nicholas" (1823, later becoming the more familiar "Twas the Night before Christmas"), Charles Dickens's *A Christmas Carol* (1843), and the cartoons of a jolly Old Santa Claus that Thomas Nast began to draw during the Civil War provided secular trappings and helped establish Christmas as a season of goodwill, presents, and child-centered familial bliss, thus making it palatable for even the most fundamentalist Protestants.

But even before all this transpired, the land that is now Illinois had not been without celebrations and rituals during the days surrounding the winter solstice. Native American communities of a thousand years ago left evidence of their observation of the solstice. And the French explorers Père Marquette and Louis Joliet must have observed Christmas when they camped in the winter of 1674 on what is now known as the South Branch of the Chicago River, even though it is probable that Marquette was too ill to officiate at a mass, as he would do the following spring at Easter for Illinois Indians in Utica. It is also possible that the first Christmas tree in Illinois was brought to Fort Dearborn at Chicago in 1803. And French settlements along the eastern bank of the Mississippi River at Fort du Chartres most certainly celebrated Christmas and the New Year, *la gui annee*, a tradition that continues to this day.

Still, celebrations rooted in historical European customs were not immediately embraced by the majority of those early Illinois settlers who were primarily of English and Scottish stock. Christmas would not become an integral part of Illinois life until later. For example, even the Episcopal bishop Philander Chase, the founder of Kenyon College in Ohio and Jubilee College in Illinois, makes little mention of Christmas in letters written to his wife during fund-raising trips in southern Illinois in the 1840s and 1850s. Uncertainty remained among Protestants as to whether they should acknowledge December 25 as a day of religious celebration, a day that on the frontier still meant to many a license to excess. Consequently, those who search Illinois history for Christmas celebrations prior to the Civil War have a difficult time unearthing evidence of them outside of Catholic enclaves.

Today, however, Christmas seems to have been always with us. It is that time of year when we expect good cheer and goodwill, a moment's respite from the year's vicissitudes, solace during difficult times. This seems especially true during times of economic hardship. Many Illinoisans remember their first Christmases during the Great Depression. Some, such as I, were born into a geography called Little Egypt, that delta-shaped portion of Illinois lying largely between the Mississippi and Ohio Rivers where shipping, coal, and timber shaped the faces of immigrant and migrant populations. For others, it was the black-earth center of the state, dominated by agriculture and characterized by stability and the boast of maintaining American values. And in the north, there seemed by the late 1890s to be all of what the other two had plus thriving cities with industry, transportation, and a reputation for putting people to work, thus attracting a population more diverse than the rest of the state put together. To many in what is called Downstate (for a lot of Chicagoans almost any place south of Roosevelt Road), Chicago was apart from rather than of Illinois. But if they did not live near St. Louis, which satisfied their occasional need for a city, Chicago was for Downstaters the place to journey to for shopping, window displays, and wonderment, particularly at Christmastime.

I grew up in the 1930s and 1940s in the city of Herrin, a community that declined during the Depression, came alive with coal and munitions production during World War II, and, like communities throughout the state, remains subject to the whims of a fickle economy. On one side of town was the Italian immigrant community, Catholic virtually to a person. On the other side was a Protestant majority of English and Scottish descent, generally Methodists, Southern Baptists, Presbyterians, or members of hardcore fundamentalist sects. I began my search for an Illinois Christmas trying to remember whether Christmas was ever brought into the sanctuary of the Southern Baptist church that I attended with my grandmother and mother. If so, it was dramatically unlike what seemed to me to be the exotic Christmas Mass attended by my Catholic friends. There was no Latin mass or abundantly visual displays of the Virgin and Child that made the Christmas story lively and filled with mystery. During the latter part of the Depression and World War II, our Southern Baptist minister adhered, as he was required to do by the tenets of his faith and his congregation, to the literal meaning of the Bible. The only embellishments on the story of the birth of Christ—related briefly and somewhat disjointedly in Matthew 1:18–25 and Luke 1:26–35 and 2:1–20—were in the rising and falling tone of the reverend's voice.

As I remember, it was only in the sanctity of our four-room coal-miner's house that Christmas became meaningful. Once the tree was up, an angel placed at the highest point, and the lights turned on, I would hurry outside, stand on the brick cobbled street, and look in awe at how the tree made our house appear a welcoming and wondrous abode. In my mind's eye it has now taken on the aura of a most resplendent crèche. On Christmas Day the magic moment continued when we opened our gifts, few in number but cherished for as long as they held together.

As was predicted from the pulpit, when I left for Decatur to attend Millikin University in 1951, I and my classmates who headed northward needed to be aware of the dangers of mingling with northern sinners. "Sinners" meant, of course, human beings who did not share the preacher's ideas. First, I became a Presbyterian. Then in Champaign I began to study the works of the philosopher George Santayana, who espoused a life of reason while valuing the art and ritual of the Catholic church. Later in Peoria I became a Congregationalist and, still later in Oak Park, the husband of a Unitarian-Universalist. A grandson is a happy celebrant of both Hanukkah and Christmas.

Even as Christmas celebrations changed in the religious venues I have experienced over time, and my understanding of religion has altered greatly from what I was taught early on, I still get caught up in the excitement of the season. The principal difference between early Christmases and those of today is not so much religious attitude as the unbridled obsession with gifts. As I write this in 2009 in my study in Ottawa, where my wife and I have spent over a decade of Christmases, I observe with not a little irony that during this past year of economic uncertainty gift giving has become almost as meaningful as it was during the Depression. Gifts are far fewer and more thoughtful and useful. As the guy who repairs the dents in my car told me last December, of all the presents he has received throughout his life, a set of wrenches from his father was by far the best.

Over the past century in Illinois, Christmas has blossomed into a season rather than a date, lasting from Thanksgiving to Epiphany. On the heels of the Depression, following pressure from national retailers who were correct in thinking that a lengthened period from Thanksgiving to Christmas would encourage people to shop longer and consume more, Franklin Delano Roosevelt approved setting Thanksgiving on the fourth Thursday of November. Thus, the day after Thanksgiving, known by many as "black Friday," when Christmas buying begins in earnest, always allows for an extra day or two of shopping between Thanksgiving and Christmas. In Illinois as elsewhere, consumption over the Christmas season is a benchmark for success in retailing. Recent attempts to make Christmas remain an economic engine led major retailers in 2009 to begin advertising Christmas sales in July.

Still, in spite of becoming a frenzied commercial event where consumers are titillated by new products and advertising, Christmas in Illinois survives as a season in which domestic intimacy intensifies and strangers unabashedly look one another in the eye, give a greeting, and smile. It is a time of quiet and contemplation. And yes, it is also a season where many fall into depression, not because of the goodwill they see around them but because they find themselves unable to join in. They, too, are affected by the season, the stasis, the pause in the momentum of things, and find themselves not able to cope with it all. The season overwhelms. We look on it and its effect on us with anticipation as well as wariness.

The intensity of the Christmas season has helped to give Illinoisans of varying religious beliefs and cultural origins reason to define for themselves and their fellow citizens what they believe in. Hannukah, Kwanzaa, Christmas—for some celebrants religious, for others secular—all cluster around the winter solstice, that time of the year in the Northern Hemisphere when waning light begins to wax; a time when the hush of snow covers prairie, woods, and cities; a time when rest and taking stock precede the promise of spring; a time to acknowledge the presence of others with gifts of the self.

This book is about Christmas celebrated in Illinois and remembered by Illinoisans; some are widely familiar as writers, photographers, and artists, but most are known only in their close-knit communities. Many articles have been written specifically for this anthology or have been discovered in archives. They are from people who learned that I was searching for stories and images through my visits in their communities, e-mails, telephone calls, or newspaper articles written about my search. Looking for Christmas in July or February makes news. People have been generous with their time, mainly because they know from their own experience that Christmas is a cultural index to where and how they live or have lived, whether they migrated or were born into the state. No matter when their words were written or images created, each person included here shares an experience and then retires respectfully from the stage as others step forth to talk about the holiday they all know as an Illinois Christmas. It is as if we were present at a rare town meeting marked by the civility we have come to expect from the season.

This is also a book about Illinois, a state first defined by the artificial boundaries of 1818 but today defined by a sense of place that makes it feel different from anywhere else in the United States. It is known as the Prairie State and the Land of Lincoln, primarily because the essence of the prairie and of the humanity that was Lincoln is palatable. Many of its citizens may agree with the noted botantist and Illinoisan Donald Culross Peattie, who wrote on April 26, 1959, in the *New York Times Magazine* that it is "[t]he Best State of the Fifty." Admitting that he would be derided by all his readers "except several million suckers (natives of this state, so called for the ugly-faced fish that feed at the bottom of its sluggish streams), and in Washington, D.C., [by his] friend Senator Paul Douglas, and [by]—wherever he is—Adlai E. Stevenson," he avowed simply, "Illinois is the best state precisely because it is so American." To Peattie, Illinois exemplifies the beauty and diversity of topography, plant life, and people that can be found elsewhere in the country. The Christmas commemorations found in this book may well do the same.

James Ballowe
OTTAWA

Christmas in Illinois History

Christmas at Kaskaskia

VIRGINIA EIFERT

Virginia Eifert edited the Living Museum, *the magazine of the Illinois State Museum, from 1939 to 1966. In 1953 she published* Three Rivers South *(1953), a historical novel about Abraham Lincoln's flatboat trip to New Orleans via the Sangamon, Illinois, and Mississippi Rivers. The first of fifteen books she would write in the next thirteen years, it employed, as does this Christmas story, her deep knowledge of Illinois and its rivers, people, and natural history.*

I t was the year 1700 in the old French town of Kaskaskia, situated on a point of land thrusting into the Mississippi in southern Illinois. Now in the chill early dusk of December, the bells in the church rang out across a wilderness of land and water to call the faithful to Christmas Eve services.

Alone and brave above the great river, Kaskaskia felt itself "an outpost of civilization and culture; in a wilderness peopled largely by unlettered savages, the civilization and religion and learning of the West had found their foothold." As the centuries passed, Kaskaskia vanished from the map, but the old town had played its part in the story of America.

Christmas in the early days of Illinois was not celebrated very extensively as we know it and observe it today. But in the French manner, modified only by the exigencies of wilderness, Christmas nevertheless came to Kaskaskia.

When the evening services were over and the candles still burned before the altar, the people, wrapped warmly against the cold of a December night, went through the snow to their log and stone homes. The fires in the big stone fireplaces were fixed for the night; bed warmers were heated to ease the chill of winter beds. And the children, before they said their prayers and dived beneath layers of homemade coverlets, carefully placed their shoes beside the hearth.

Christmas at Kaskaskia. Two hundred and fifty years ago, what did the Christ Child bring to the hopeful children of that outpost of old France along the Mississippi? No one knows. But in the old records of goods sold in shops, there were many things imported from France, as well as utilitarian items made locally. Perhaps in a boy's shoe there might have been a pair of silver knee-buckles; there might have been a bright Paris ribbon for little sister; there could have been maple sugar candies wrapped carefully in soft paper saved from France; perhaps little white cakes, the *petit gateaux*, which even then may have been loved by children whether they lived in Paris or Kaskaskia.

And on Christmas morning, there was the same shining joy over the gifts, meager though they might be, as there always is joy among children at Christmas. The day, however, was not celebrated with merriment, but with solemn mass at the church. Merry-making was reserved for New Year's and for Twelfth Night, when special cakes celebrated the end of the Christmas season.

But there may be no records of Christmas at Kaskaskia. More important events were recorded in the long story of the old town.

Kaskaskia saw the coming and going of adventurers and explorers and the makers of history. It saw three flags wave over its hundreds of houses—the flag of France, in the days when the Illinois shore was French and the Missouri shore was Spanish; it saw the coming of the British flag, and saw it fall before George Rogers Clark and his American soldiers who brought the American flag to Illinois and left it planted there forever.

But Kaskaskia did not stay forever. Year by year when the floods receded, the point of land had grown smaller. The legislature and seat of government were moved in 1818 to Vandalia, for the river was devouring Kaskaskia. In 1880–81 the Mississippi cut across the neck of land, and Kaskaskia became an island. Year after year as the floods came, more of Kaskaskia vanished. One by one, the old houses slipped into the swirling brown water; fewer people remained to defy the river, though some remained until 1898; and a few lived on the bluffs out of reach of the water. In 1906, a single chimney stood on a bank above the river—and when the chimney fell down under the relentless river's rising current, that was the end of Kaskaskia, whose church bells on a Christmas night once rang out across the wilderness.

Christmas on the Cache

JOHN W. ALLEN

Having the earliest settlements in the state, deep southern Illinois is rich with accounts of early Christmases. No one knew them better than John W. Allen. Allen, who eventually became president of the Illinois State Historical Society, was born in Broughton in Hamilton County in 1887. His father, a farmer, moved the family to near Shawneetown in Gallatin County, then to what was known as the Douglas House on the border of Saline and Gallatin Counties. As Allen's friend Irving Dillard of Collinsville says in his foreword to Allen's Legends and Lore of Southern Illinois, *Allen remembered a Christmas at the Douglas House when he was five. There, in front of "its great fireplace," Allen "received his first orange and a little red wagon." The family later moved close to villages with names such as Hardscrabble and Texas City in Saline County. After a long career as a school teacher and administrator in Saline County, Allen settled his own family near Carbondale, where he taught at Southern Illinois University.*

The earliest account found about Christmas and the manner in which it was spent in southern Illinois, outside of the French settlements along the Mississippi, appeared in a paper that was published in London (England) in 1828. It tells how John James Audubon, the great naturalist, spent Christmas Day of 1810 near the mouth of the Cache River where it joins the Ohio about six miles above Cairo.

Audubon and a Frenchman named Ferdinand Rozier had left Henderson, Kentucky, a few days earlier with a keelboat-load of merchandise, consisting of three hundred barrels of whiskey, sundry dry goods, and gunpowder. Audubon was on his way to Sainte Genevieve, Missouri, where he and a man named Herrick planned to establish a business.

When they reached the mouth of the Cache on December 23, Audubon and Rozier came across some other travelers there. They also found about twenty-five families of Shawnee Indians who were camped to gather nuts and to hunt. From the travelers and the Indians, Audubon and Rozier learned that the Mississippi was covered with thick ice and that boats could not use it. They therefore decided to remain at the Shawnee camp.

The second day after his arrival—that is, on the morning of December 25—Audubon tells that he was awakened early in the morning by the activities of the Shawnee. He arose at once and found that a canoe with a half-dozen squaws and as many warriors was about ready to leave for a large lake on the Kentucky side for the purpose of killing swans.

Audubon was given permission to accompany the Indians in the canoe. He went along, as he states, "well-equipped with ammunition and whiskey." He relates that the task of paddling the canoe across the river was performed by the squaws and that "the hunters laid down and positively slept during the whole passage." When they reached the Kentucky side, the squaws made the canoe secure and began to gather nuts. The hunters made their way through the "thick and thin" to the lake, the thick and thin being the thickets of small cottonwood trees and occasional lagoons that bordered the river.

In a short time, they reached the lake, where they saw swans "by the hundreds, of a white or rich cream color—either dipping their black bills in the water or . . . floating along and basking in the sunshine." Three of the Indians passed around to the other side of the lake and three remained on the side nearest the river. Audubon joined one of the groups, and all hid themselves behind trees. When the hunters on either side of the lake alarmed them, the swans would arise and fly to the other side, where the hunters hidden there would take careful aim and fire. Alternating, the hunters repeated the process until a large number of birds were killed.

In describing the situation, Audubon says: "I saw these beautiful birds floating on the water, their backs downward, their heads under the surface and their legs in the air, struggling in the last agonies of life, to the number of at least fifty—their beautiful skins all intended for ladies of Europe."

When the sun was nearly even with the tops of the trees, "a conch was sounded and the squaws shortly appeared, dragging the canoe, and went about in quest of the dead game." All was "transported to the River's edge and landed upon the Illinois shore before dark."

"The fires were lighted—each man ate his mess of pecans and bear fat, and stretched himself out, with his feet near the small heap of coals intended for the night. The females began their work; it was their duty to skin the birds. I observed them for some time and then retired to rest, very well satisfied with the sport of this day—the twenty-fifth of December."

Skins as a Circulating Medium

R. O. WHITE

Linda Hanabarger of Ramsey, the editor of the Fayette County Genealogical and Historical Society, contributed this story of an incident in Bond County that typifies the way many Illinoisans in the territory celebrated Christmas with high jinks.

From the time the first settlements were made in what is now Bond County until the close of the War of 1812, money was scarcely ever seen. Skins of the mink, muskrat, raccoon, and deer composed the circulating medium of the country. Tobacco, powder, lead, and whiskey were the principal articles purchased, and the merchant or grocery-keeper, when asked the price of any of his goods, replied by stating a number of skins per pound or gallon.

A story is told of a party of fellows on a Christmas spree, who, finding themselves about out of whiskey, and not having the wherewithal to replenish, hit upon the following expedient to obtain a supply: They went out one night to a little grocery, having one raccoon skin with them. This paid for whiskey enough to furnish them all a drink or two around, including the proprietor, who of course was fond of the article and imbibed rather freely, soon becoming hilarious from its effects. The party observed this, and each one, on placing the liquor to his lips, merely tasted it; but the grocery-keeper, whenever it came his turn, took a good drink; consequently objects soon began to assume a confused appearance to his vision. This was just what they wanted, and getting him "about right," as they expressed it, one of them slipped back to where the pile of skins lay, took one, and put it through a large crack in the wall of the hut, to the outside; then going out at the door he went round, took up the skin, and after waiting a few minutes came in—being saluted by the others as a fresh arrival—and presented his raccoon skin in payment for a certain amount of whiskey. This offer was readily accepted, the whiskey measured out, and the skin thrown back on the heap with the rest. This feat was repeated every few minutes till they obtained all the whiskey they wanted, having actually sold the grocery-keeper his own raccoon skin six or seven times in a few hours. After the close of the war, money was brought into the country and gradually took the place of skins.

The Drunken Turkey

HENRY LUSTER TO WILLIAM LANE CARSON

This story, told by Henry Luster to William Lane Carson in the 1840s and recorded by Linda Hanabarger in the Vandalia Leader-Union, *reveals that some frontiersmen were not so sportsmanlike when it came to hunting for Christmas dinner.*

Wild turkeys were very numerous, and in the fall the gobblers would gang together. Old Henry and his brother, Phil, learned where a gang of forty roosted.

They went in the night, and under the tree scattered three pecks of shelled corn. In the morning, the turkeys would get down and eat the corn. They did this for some time, as corn was only a picayune, or six and a half cents, a bushel.

The week before Christmas they got three gallons of whiskey and put the corn to soak until all the whiskey was absorbed. They then put it under the tree, as usual.

The next morning they secreted themselves and awaited results. After the corn was about all consumed, one big fellow commenced to strut and gobble and promenade around the stick. He was soon joined by others, and at last they all got to gobbling and strutting and mixed up like an old Virginia Reel.

Soon a fight got up, and the feathers and leaves flew—the like he had never seen. They ran up, clubs in hands, and began to murder the drunken gobblers. At last they had them all killed but one, and he came at them with all the vengeance of an angry devil. After quite a fight, they got him, too.

After resting a while, they brought their Dearborn wagon, loaded them, took them to town, and sold them—getting groceries enough to last them over the holidays.

Christmas in Joseph Smith's Nauvoo

JOSEPH SMITH

In this brief diary entry, Joseph Smith describes a celebration among the Mormons on Christmas Day in Nauvoo. While he was a friend and bodyguard of Joseph Smith, Orrin Porter Rockwell had a reputation for conviviality uncommon in the Mormon community.

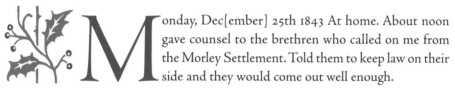

Monday, Dec[ember] 25th 1843 At home. About noon gave counsel to the brethren who called on me from the Morley Settlement. Told them to keep law on their side and they would come out well enough.

About 2 o'c[loc]k about 50 couple[s] sat down at my table to dine. While I was eating[,] my scribe called on me to solemnize the Marriage of Doct[or] Levi Richards and Sarah Griffiths, but as I could not leave I referred the subject to Pres[i]d[en]t B[righam] Young who married them.

A large party supped at my house and spent the evening /in a most cheerful and friendly manner/ in Music, Dancing, &c. During the festivities a man apparently drunk, with his hair long and falling over his shoulders come in and acted like a Missourian. I commanded the Capt[ain] of the police to put him out of doors. In the scuffle, I looked him full in the face and to my great surprize and Joy untold I discovered it was Orrin Porter Rockwell, just arrived from a years imprisonment in M[iss]o[uri].

A Christmas Spree

PRESLEY G. DONALDSON

Because of the unrestrained activities of many Christmas revelers, the word spree *became almost synonymous with Christmas on the frontier. Fayette County residents were no exception.*

As many men have written little histories and as many of my friends have solicited me to write a brief history, I will give the public a partial history in plain home chat, from my earliest recollection to the present date—1908. I will speak largely of my boyhood days and the wildness of the country sixty years ago; I will speak of the wild animals that inhabited the country for thirty years of my youthful life. I was born and raised in the state of Illinois, in Fayette County, on the headwaters of Hurricane Creek.

I will now give a brief history of myself from the time I was twenty years old until I was thirty-five. I must acknowledge that I was a spreeing man fifteen years. I never was any hand to go into a saloon and stay. I was a man who was generally up and doing and never ran out of a job even when I was drinking. If I saw that I was going to run out of a job I would get into a pinching racket to see who could pinch a piece of the other first. I have been pinched until I was black and blue. Now reader, do you suppose we were mad when we were pinching? No, verily not, we were ready to drink together any hour of the day. George Lovegrove, Charlie Watkins, Ed Dickerson, Jerome Daniels, Franklin Freeman, and many others were my chums at this time and we had some great times. I want to tell you about a Christmas spree we had. Franklin Freeman, Ed Dickerson, and Charlie Watkins left Ramsey well supplied with whiskey and started for Charlie Watkins's to eat a Christmas supper where they had a turkey gobbler cooked. But before we got to the supper something happened on the road that I must tell. Old Man Cline overtook us just at the top of Ramsey Hill. He was riding a little black mule. We acted neighborly with Mr. Cline and gave him a dram. The first thing we knew, Charlie Watkins, Franklin Freeman, and myself were up behind Mr. Cline on the poor little mule. Reader, think of four good-sized men on one little mule. Ed Dickerson was not idle all this time. He was loading his gun. The little mule was trudging along just about the middle of the hill; about this time Dickerson shot off the gun. The poor mule tried to jump but fell down and men, mule and all went rolling down the hill. Dickerson had more fun than all the rest. I wish I had a picture of all hands when the mule fell. Friends, I leave it to your imagination and I am not afraid of you overdrawing the picture. Mr. Cline started home and, no doubt, was feeling pretty good because he had escaped.

We went on to the supper and found they had the turkey cooked and the table nicely set. The women had started in to have a nice time and everything was nice until we men arrived on the scene of action. We grabbed that gobbler, tore him in four pieces bare-handed and made a perfect mess of everything. We ate the supper, kissed the girls and women—and what do you think we did next?—went straight back to Ramsey to lay on a little more kindling wood. We then scattered out, went home about ten o'clock that night and dreamed of sky-blue lizards and red-hot reptiles.

Christmas the Same as Any Other Day

OWEN W. MUELDER

This history of Christmas at Galesburg's Knox College by Owen Muelder, best known for his research on the Illinois Underground Railroad, indicates the attitude of the keepers of the faith toward celebrating Christmas before the Civil War.

 I often recall during the holiday season a story my father took great pleasure in retelling about the no-nonsense approach the founders of Knox College adopted in regard to Christmas Day. He usually told this story with a wry smile. But first I should present a little background.

The end of the 1832 Black Hawk War signaled to many Americans living in the East that the land between the Illinois River and the Mississippi River was finally safe for settlement. In 1837, the Reverend George Washington Gale established in western Illinois the town of Galesburg and Knox College, almost simultaneously. Gale, a Presbyterian minister, had previously established the Oneida Institute in upstate New York. This school was strongly associated with the so-called Great Revival or Second Great Awakening, a religious movement that had a profound impact on the nation in the nineteenth century. On the Illinois frontier, however, Gale was willing to coexist with Congregationalists under an arrangement called the "Plan of Union." These Protestant pioneers followed strict religious practices and codes of behavior, vehemently supported the Temperance movement, and openly advocated antislavery points of view.

The smaller number of Hoosiers and families from southern Illinois and states below the Ohio River, who had come into western Illinois earlier, thought these easterners were very strange and snobbish. They soon came to believe that Gale's colony was mostly composed of self-righteous, teetotalling, troublemaking abolitionists. In fact, it was not long before Galesburg was known throughout the state as a community where fugitive slaves might be hidden and where anyone thought to be consuming "spirits" would be ostracized. The school's first buildings were simple and plain; teachers conducted classes in rooms that were a challenge to keep warm in the winter. The community's founding fathers and church deacons were serious-minded individuals. The Fourth of July, for instance, was not celebrated with parades and frivolity but was more likely to be organized around an antislavery gathering. The administrators of Knox College took an equally rigid approach to the observance of Christmas. Earnest Elmo Calkins, the author of *They Broke the Prairie*, in a fascinating account of the early history of Galesburg and Knox College, states that December 24 and 25 "had no sentimental associations . . . for these New England Christians did not celebrate Christmas." The first president of Knox College, Hiram H. Kellogg, assumed that students would attend classes on Christ's birthday, and the college's second president, the controversial abolitionist Jonathan Blanchard, who arrived in Galesburg from Cincinnati in the mid-1840s, expected the same attendance requirement on Christmas Day. This stern policy exemplified the founders' belief that a virtuous life could best be achieved through the discipline of pious perseverance.

However, in the early 1850s, a daring group of students hatched a plan that attempted to change that tradition, hoping to bring to the dark days of the winter solstice a few hours of cheer. Christmas, they believed, should not be treated same as any other day. On December 24, 1851, they unsuccessfully attempted to stop classes from taking place the next morning by hiding the bell, removing the keys to the recitation rooms, and locking the doors after having sealed the window latches. This behavior was deemed sufficiently reprehensible by the school's authorities that the incident was investigated and the proceedings were recorded in the faculty minutes.

Although professors delivered prepared lectures to students, it was more often the case that young scholars were asked to read aloud each day from classic texts. The term "recitation room" was more commonly used than "classroom." Rote memorization was required and students had to deliver, without reference to notes or an outline, a Latin conjugation, a famous speech, or a long poem. In the nineteenth century, educators believed in very little classroom discussion between teachers and pupils, which is so commonplace in modern-day education. It was believed then that daily recitation not only encouraged lasting memory of a given topic but also honed the development of oral expression.

Knox College did not have as yet a large bell hanging from a substantial bell tower. Instead, a bell was rung by hand in the hallways of buildings where both recitation rooms and dormitory rooms were located in the same structure. Therefore, students knew that if they could snatch the hand bell and hide it, no one would hear the regular daily summons to class.

If these students' daring escapade had succeeded, the first thing that would have been altered in the regular school routine was chapel. The college catalog of 1851 read:

> The first half-hour of each day is appropriated to devotional exercises, and to lectures by the President on various moral and religious subjects, on which, as well as on the worship of God on the Sabbath, all the members of the Institution are expected to attend. The discipline is designed to be parental, and conducted on Gospel principles.

Nearly all of the faculty at Knox in those days would have been outraged by anyone who attempted to disrupt the community's daily religious duty. Nine days after the students' failed effort to have an unscheduled Christmas holiday, a committee consisting of Mr. S. Ferris (a founder and trustee), the faculty president, and six professors issued a report that indicated ten students were called before the investigating committee to explain their possible involvement in planning the caper. A student named Babbit, during his cross-examination, admitted that he had heard fellow students discussing the idea of locking "the recitation rooms but he did not feel under obligation to give their names." Another student by the name of Hinkley testified that classmates McReynolds, Davis, and Hall had acted suspiciously but "he [Hinkley] did not know who took the bell, or plugged the window, or who had connexions with the business."

Indeed, each student who was questioned said that he was not culpable and could not say who was responsible. It seems that before these young men were called into the hearing room, they must have agreed not to implicate anyone who might have been involved. Therefore, the school's officials were left with only denials and no hard evidence to prove who was guilty.

In 1859, the college finally relented and a two-day Christmas break was permitted. In the following year when fall classes began, the printed college calendar showed a recess for the holidays. Even so, Christmas celebrations at Knox College and in the town of Galesburg remained low-key affairs until after the Civil War. According to Calkins, it was not until 1871 that "the young people of the Old First Church announced they were going to have a tree for the children of the Sunday school, and did so without breaking any bones." By then, the railroads had brought into the town a more diverse population, and the influx of Germans and Swedes had most likely influenced the community to gradually embrace what we now think of as a traditional Christmas celebration.

My first- and second-hand impressions of Christmas at Knox go back nearly eighty-five years. My father, the historian H. R. Muelder, graduated from Knox College in 1927 and after graduate school joined the college's history department in 1931. He later served as the school's academic dean for eleven years, and following his retirement he was the college historian until his death in 1988. I graduated from Knox in 1963 and have held various administrative posts at the school since 1968.

Bringing in the Yule Log at the Morton Arboretum, by Jim Nachel

CHRISTMAS IN ILLINOIS HISTORY ✦ ✦ ✦ ✦ ✦ ✦ ✦ ✦ ✦ ✦ ✦ ✦ ✦ ✦ ✦ ✦ ✦ ✦

During most of my father's career at Knox, Christmastime was festive. Although students were never on campus during Christmas itself, prior to the holiday recess, students and faculty would frequently go caroling together around town. Many students put up lights, small Christmas trees, and other holiday decorations in the suites of their residence halls. The choir and madrigal singers performed concerts on campus and throughout the Galesburg community. The English professor Howard Wilson read from Dylan Thomas's "A Child's Christmas in Wales" close to a roaring fireplace in the Student Union. This setting helped recall the Yule Log, with its historic connections to northern Europe's winter festivals. Occasionally, members of the Knox community played Santa Claus at Christmas gatherings for the children of school employees. I clearly remember these and many other Christmas activities from my childhood well into my own undergraduate days at Knox, but in the late 1960s, Knox adopted a new academic calendar, still followed, that ended the fall term before Thanksgiving and started the winter term after New Year's Day. Consequently, Christmas is virtually invisible at Knox now, with only a holiday luncheon party held in mid-December. In addition, Knox College, like many other colleges and universities across the country, has, over the last several decades, taken a neutral stance towards recognizing any religion's celebratory activities. Even a large and beautiful wreath that for years hung over the entrance to the College's "Old Main" no longer adorns the building in December, despite the fact that using circular green arrangements was originally a folk practice of pre-Christian Germanic peoples honoring the winter solstice.

Too Much Spirit

Christmas of 1860 Featured Sleigh Accidents, Brawl, Shooting

TARA McCLELLAN McANDREW

As this account of Christmas in Springfield shows, rowdiness during Christmas was not limited to frontier communities in deep southern Illinois.

In the 1860s, Christmas wasn't the megaholiday it is today. While there were similarities to today's celebration, there were some big differences. In the days preceding December 25, 1860, the *Illinois State Journal* had several ads touting local stores' holiday gift options, such as gold and silver watches, "plain, chaste and hair bracelets, coral, lava, mosale and cameo sets," books, hair-braided jewelry (in 280 designs), photographs, handkerchiefs, and more.

For their last Christmas in Springfield, Mary Todd Lincoln must have bought handkerchiefs for her boys, as well as Lincoln, according to "The Personal Finances of Abraham Lincoln" by Harry Pratt (Abraham Lincoln Association, 1943). It says that on December 24, 1860, someone from the Lincoln family (the book says Mary did most of the shopping there) bought four silk children's handkerchiefs, four linen handkerchiefs, and three silk "gents'" handkerchiefs from John Williams and Company, a store on the north side of the downtown square. They totaled $3.13.

Today, the entire city practically shuts down on Christmas Eve and Christmas, but that wasn't the case then. In fact, a highly touted presentation on "The Grand Historical Illustrations of Dr. Kane's Artic [*sic*] Expedition: In Search of Sir John Franklin," by W. H. Paul, was debuting on Christmas Eve at Cook's Hall (downtown on the square). Its highlight would be a large painting "vividly portraying the sublime wonders of the Polar World," the December 21, 1860, *Journal* ad said.

On Christmas Day, some businesses operated as usual, as evidenced by an ad in the *Journal* that day: "Great Sale of Furs—The ladies are requested to remember the great sale of fine furs which begins to day at Tripp's auction room. . . ."

While the newspaper closed for the day, it marked the holiday in many ways. First, it printed all of Clement C. Moore's poem, "'Twas the Night before Christmas," on the front page on Christmas Day, along with the part of Charles Dickens's *A Christmas Carol*, titled "Bob Cratchit's Dinner."

On another page, it printed an article about Christmas customs, including the hanging of mistletoe, which it attributed to the Druids. "But the mistletoe . . . once brought a blush to the cheek and merry laughter to the lips of our foremothers years ago," said the December 25 *Journal*. "There is a custom, dating back to the dim obscurity of a Roman province, which a well-known writer speaks of as follows: 'The custom longest preserved was the hanging up of a bush of mistletoe in the hall, with the charm attached to it, that the maid who was not kissed under it at Christmas would not be married in that year.' This natural and very agreeable superstition still prevails. It would be a good idea to introduce it into Springfield. It would be attractive to the misses, and we suppose they would not object. . . ."

On Christmas Day, some Springfield families headed for the downtown "Public Square" for sleigh riding. "Never did the streets of this city present a more attractive and brilliant appearance than on Christmas day," the December 27 *Journal* said, "as the dashing cavalcade of sleighs went whirling around the public square, the musical cadence of the merry bells keeping time to the monotonous tramp of the spirited horses. Joyous and happy shouts of laughter saluted the ear everywhere as the many loads of pleasure seekers went gliding by. . . ."

Not all of the shouts were joyous.

On the same page, the *Journal* had articles about sleigh-riding accidents. Grandma didn't get run over by a reindeer, but little Johnny got run over by a sleigh. "The son of Gen. John Cook was run over by a sleigh on the public square, Christmas Day," the *Journal* said. "He was, however, not injured, but rather indignant. The little fellow has plenty of nerve."

Yet another child was run over by a sleigh that day. According to the *Journal*, the little boy had just purchased a sled and was crossing the street with it, when a sleigh driver, "who was guilty of inexcusable carelessness," ran him over. "The boy escaped with but a few injuries." If the driver had stopped in time for police to arrest him, the paper said, he would have been "sternly dealt with by the law."

Ah, the Christmas spirit had just begun to ring in. There also was a barroom brawl that afternoon, according to the December 27 *Journal*. It said that "two young men from the country" were charged in court the day before with "being disorderly and with indulging in too great an extent their merrymaking propensities on Christmas Day. It seems these two gay young men about town (Joseph Gamble and Thomas Benton Tomlinson) went into (Louis) Welk's and becoming rather quarrelsome in their cups, had a regular set to, resulting in very little damage except broken noses and bloody faces, and a general demolition of glass ware. Welk, in endeavoring to part them, had to adopt something more than moral suasion. An officer entering about that time, the whole three were arrested. . . ."

And the most bizarre Christmas Day incident of all that year ended in a shooting. The December 27 *Illinois State Journal* said that a man named Gus Loyd, "who is well known to many of our citizens," went to the livery stable of "Mr. Cone" on Christmas, "whilst under the influence of liquor." Once there, he "bit the ear off a favorite cat, the pet of the establishment." One of the stable's workers, Bell Watkins, got mad at Loyd. "High words passed between him and Loyd, which resulted in an agreement to fight on the prairie. They both mounted horses and started for the country. When they arrived on the 'field of honor,' before Watkins was able to dismount, Loyd drew a revolver and fired three consecutive shots at him, one passing through his hat, the other grazing his body."

Loyd was taken into custody immediately.

Christmas in 1863:
A Civil War Soldier's Account

JOHN B. REID

Kevin Kaegy of the Bond County Historical Society introduced this Civil War soldier's letter home with this background:

———————————————

A Greenville resident, Major John B. Reid of the 130ᵗʰ Illinois Infantry wrote more than one hundred letters home during the American Civil War. Later promoted to colonel, he attained the highest rank of any soldier to serve from Bond County.

During Christmas of 1863, he and about two hundred other Bond County men were camped out near the Gulf of Mexico. They were making preparation for the ill-fated assault up the Red River Valley through Louisiana and Texas in the spring of 1864.

John Reid's letters home help to tell the story that our local men lived through in those troubled times. We need to remember that this was not written by a distinguished gray-bearded gentleman but rather by a thirty-three-year-old father of four children. He was a devoted husband and a deeply religious man. Surrounded by the tragedy of war, he wondered if he would survive. Fortunately, he did survive and was for many years one of Greenville's most prominent citizens. He and his wife had six more children after the war for a total of ten.

Colonel Reid died on Christmas Day, December 25, 1907, at the age of seventy-seven. He was buried in Montrose Cemetery, and his funeral was one of the largest ever held here. Reid's family home still stands at 504 South Prairie Street. Extensively remodeled in the 1950s by Francis Rinderer, it is the two-story eastern section of the Bond County Health Department.

On December 26, 1912, Mrs. Reid let Will Carson start reprinting her husband's letters. By virtue of his rank, he was in a position to know many of the inside details of the movements of the army. A few years ago, Nelda Anthony retyped these letters from the Greenville Advocate *files for the Bond County Historical Society.*

Decrows Point
Matagorda, Texas
December 25, 1863

Dear Wife and Children,

I wish you all a Merry Christmas; as for myself I have spent as pleasant a day as could be expected. The day proved to be warm and pleasant and a great number of the men went bathing. I did not indulge myself, but those that did said the water was very comfortably warm and the salt water seemed to give them all fine appetites for the enjoyment of their hardtack, coffee, and mutton.

After our dress parade, which was our only duty of the morning, I in company with a few more officers went on board a ship to a splendid dinner. We had soup, baked fish, turkey, pudding pie, nuts, and raisins. It was indeed a treat to us all and served as only a first-class steamboat cook can serve.

I trust that you and the dear ones have enjoyed the day and it would have been much more pleasant to have been with you, but God orders it otherwise. I hope the sheets of small currency reached you in time for this day as the children should see that father did not forget them while so far away. I suppose Mr. Murdock was with his happy family for their Christmas dinner and I know it must have been a great comfort to them to have him there after so long an absence.

This afternoon Captain Patrick and myself spent most of the afternoon boxing up shells. We are going to send them to New Orleans the first chance we have where they will be looked after by some friend of his; some early date in spring he hopes to go home and will take them with him to his home in Belleville. There he will take out his part and will rebox and ship those intended for you. I hope you keep up a cheerful spirit and when you feel that your lot is a hard one just look around a little and you will be able to see many others who are worse off than you.

Ed Dewey and I are living together and have quite a serviceable place made of cotton bales, the floor covered with a carpet of salt grass, on one side is our bed and on the other we have a table made out of an old box and covered with newspapers. On the table we have a testament, a clothes brush, a tooth brush, Casey's Army Tactics, a looking glass, thread, needles, etc. Across the tent, for we call it a tent, being covered with a canvas top, we have a stout line on which we hang our clothes. Take it all in all we think we are quite neat housekeepers but the place doesn't look like a house of any real lady housekeeper.

We have not heard of any chance of leaving here, but will keep hoping that some orders will soon come. The monotony of this remaining idle in one place is very trying and we would rather be on the march or in a real fight than doing nothing. You must write me all the particulars of your Christmas; I know that you wished I was with you often during the day and perhaps are now writing to me—after the busy day is over and our sweet children are safely asleep. God bless them and watch over them this night is the prayer of their loving and absent father.

Among our party on the steamer today were four ladies that had just arrived from Rio Grande, on the way north. It seemed good to see some real well-dressed and intelligent women. The Rio Grande divides this state from Mexico and our troops are at Brownsville, opposite Matamoras, Mexico, a city of twenty-five thousand inhabitants and said to be a very interesting place to strangers. I hope to be able to make a trip over there before we get away from this locality.

Jimmy and Ed Dewey, as well as others best acquainted with you, ask to join me in wishing you all a "Merry Christmas." Kiss the children for me.

Your Loving and Absent Husband,
John B. Reid

How Christmas Came to Clover Lawn

MARCIA D. YOUNG

A professional historian with a doctorate from Harvard, Marcia D. Young has been the site manager of the David Davis Mansion in Bloomington for the past two decades. Here she provides insight into the Christmases that preceded the elaborate Victorian celebrations of the Gilded Age.

Each December, the David Davis Mansion in Bloomington is decorated for an elaborate Victorian Christmas. The mansion, a state historic site, was originally built in the 1870s as a private home for Judge David Davis and his wife Sarah. They called their estate Clover Lawn in recognition of the little plant that grew abundantly around their property. Today, the site's annual celebration, known as "Christmas at Clover Lawn," tells the story of the way that Americans celebrated Christmas during the years following the judge's death (1890–1917).

There is, however, another holiday tale that has never been told until now. It is the story of how David and Sarah Davis celebrated Christmas in their old Bloomington farmhouse, which Abraham Lincoln often visited during his circuit-riding years. Although the farmhouse was moved to make way for the present mansion, the story contained within its walls helps to explain how Bloomington residents first celebrated Christmas long before it evolved into an elaborate and fashionable holiday in the late Gilded Age. The Davis family's little-known story mirrors the way that Christmas in America became what it is today.

David Davis achieved prominence as a lawyer, businessman, U.S. Supreme Court judge, and U.S. senator from Illinois, and his home reflects the fame that he attained nationally as a result of his friendship with Abraham Lincoln. The two men met for the first time in 1835, beginning a personal, professional, and political relationship that would last for thirty years.

But it is Sarah Davis, the judge's wife, who is at the heart of this Christmas-in-Bloomington story. Sarah was a Yankee girl who brought New England traditions to Bloomington when she arrived as a young bride in 1839. Born in Lenox, in western Massachusetts, she grew up in a world dominated by Puritans—religious reformers

*David Davis
Mansion at
Christmas, by
Dave Wilson*

whose ancestors had banned the celebration of Christmas during the seventeenth
and eighteenth centuries. What upset Puritans the most were not the feast days associated with Catholic celebrations in Europe but the fact that Christmas was still
celebrated (in the major cities of the eastern United States) as it had been in medieval times—by marauding gangs of juveniles engaged in unruly and socially disrup-
tive behavior. By the late eighteenth century, Christmas in New England was again
being celebrated as a "season of misrule." Southerners shot off their guns to mark the
holiday, and masked merrymakers in the middle-Atlantic states wandered about the
countryside with drawn swords.

Worried by this growing social unrest, America's religious and literary figures began calling for the creation of a national holiday that would transform Christmas from a lawless public spectacle into a child-centered, home-based celebration. The holiday that seemed to fit these requirements best was Thanksgiving. Celebrating a national day of Thanksgiving seemed the perfect way to evoke nostalgic memories of the past, emphasize family piety, and create traditions that would bind the nation together. By the early nineteenth century, New Englanders began observing Thanksgiving as a pious celebration of home and family life. But the holiday was slow to catch on outside New England, and when Sarah Davis arrived in Bloomington, she despaired of finding anyone who was celebrating the day. "Illinois," she wrote in 1854, "[is] so new a state and a day of Thanksgiving so new to us that we cannot expect our children to entertain the same feelings that the children of New England parents do."

Sarah was undaunted by what she found, however, and soon began introducing New England's Thanksgiving traditions to her young children, as well as to her new friends in Bloomington. By the 1870s, she was serving all the traditional Thanksgiving foods that had been served during her childhood—turkey and chicken, along with gravy and cranberry sauce. These were not the foods that the original Pilgrim settlers or their Indian neighbors had eaten, of course; instead, they were the foods available in New England before the weather was cold enough to butcher pigs and cattle. Sarah Davis even served two roasted turkeys on Thanksgiving Day in the 1870s: she carved one, while her son, sitting at the head of the table, carved the other. Sarah also loved serving chicken pie, which was as popular then as roasted turkey is today. One version, called "Connecticut Thanksgiving Chicken Pie," featured boned, stewed chicken and butter baked in a puff pastry crust. She also served creamed onions and celery—the latter a mark of status because it could only be cultivated in hothouses and was considered an expensive delicacy. For dessert, Sarah served both apple and mincemeat pies. Mincemeat, a Victorian delicacy, was a mixture of finely chopped raisins, apples, spices, suet, nuts, lean beef, and brandy or rum. Although some of her Puritan ancestors may have outlawed the dish because it contained alcohol, Sarah was not deterred. Household guides of the day recommended that cooks should begin preparing the mincemeat as early as possible—up to a month in advance, if practical. Some housewives served as many as five different kinds of pies, many of which were filled with fruit, but Sarah seems to have preferred mincemeat, perhaps because she associated it fondly with her childhood.

Compared with Thanksgiving, Christmas was not much of a holiday in Bloomington during the settlers' early years there. The only people who celebrated the day were families sharing a meal together or individuals (probably from the South) who held shooting contests in public or (as one old settler recalled) fired off anvils, "the only kind of cannon known here in those days."

Another popular holiday tradition during the early years was the custom of hosting and attending open houses on New Year's Day (a tradition that involved public parties and the liberal consumption of alcohol). By 1840, when Sarah arrived, Bloomington residents (like their counterparts all over the United States) were beginning to celebrate both New Year's Day *and* Christmas Day, by calling on one another: "Our population is not much given to visiting though they generously indulge themselves a little in the Christmas and New Year's Holidays," Sarah wrote to her sister Fanny in January 1840.

A decade later, during the late 1840s and early 1850s, when New England families were beginning to celebrate Christmas more frequently than New Year's Day, Sarah began paying more attention to Christmas as well. Yet, the kind of Christmas that she celebrated in the 1850s bore little resemblance to the fashionable Victorian celebrations of a later generation. For Sarah, Christmas was primarily a time for exchanging simple gifts with relatives. Expressing the sentiments of a frugal, New England–born housewife, she wrote in November 1847: "I am really at a loss to tell you what presents I would like to give. I would like to give Cornelia [her sister] something useful . . . like a muslin dress . . . if you see one that is pretty." She then continued enumerating the other practical gifts on her list: a purse for her sister Fanny, a genteel lace cap appropriate for her elderly mother, six pairs of cotton stockings for her brother's baby, a whittling knife for her son George, a box of tooth powder for her niece and nephew, a cake of sweet soap for her older brother, and a cloak and bonnet for herself. She concluded in a deferential manner, characteristic of a properly bred, Victorian wife: "I should prefer your not getting these articles dear D[avid]—if you feel troubled at the commission."

Young people in Bloomington also celebrated Christmas just as earlier generations had in previous decades (1820s and 1830s)—by going on sleigh rides with people their own age. Reminiscing about the years when he and Sarah were courting in Lenox at Christmastime, David wrote to Sarah from Washington, D.C., in December 1867: "Sleigh bells have been tingling night and day for several days and they remind me of my young days in Mass[tts] when it was bliss to get you in a sleigh and ride with you to the tintinnabulation of the bells. . . ."

By the time of the Civil War, many Americans, including Sarah Davis, had begun celebrating a form of Christmas that seems more familiar to us today. Victorian authors, illustrators, and reformers had finally managed to invent nearly all the trappings of a modern Christmas—gift giving (toys and candy for children), Christmas trees, seasonal foods, and Santa Claus. During the 1860s, Bloomington's *Daily Pantagraph* began running advertisements for Christmas gifts, which were supposed to be delivered by Santa Claus himself. One such ad, placed by the Bloomington merchants Maxwell and Ridlehuber on December 20, 1861, proclaimed, "Look out for Santa Claus! Holiday Presents. A Splendid Lot of Gift Books! Annuals! Bibles, Albums, Dressing Cases, etc." An earlier ad on December 11 boasted that John Holloway "has been filling his store jam full of toys, confectionery, and other fancy articles for the holidays."

Sarah Davis's letters from the 1860s also contain more frequent references to Christmas, and Santa Claus's name appears for the first time, as well. On December 27, 1866, she wrote to David (who was spending Christmas in Washington, D.C.) that the family had had a Merry Christmas but had decided "to dispense with the hanging up of stockings for 'Santa Claus.'" Although Sarah had apparently adopted the new custom of hanging stockings on Christmas Eve, she may have decided that since her children were now older (George was in his twenties and Sallie, her early teens), she could simply place the gifts (she called them "parcels") in a large basket in her room on "the night before Christmas" and then wait to distribute them when breakfast was over. After more than a decade of gift giving, Sarah and her family were now exchanging more expensive gifts—money, gloves, cologne, a cigar case (for son George), books, jewelry, sewing items, and a watch case. The gifts were reflective perhaps of the Davis family's increasing prosperity and of their adult children's more mature needs. The judge was also more interested in giving gifts than he had been previously. His enthusiasm is evident in a letter Sarah wrote to Fanny the day after Christmas, 1864. The judge had been confined at home with a carbuncle and had commissioned Sarah to run errands for him. With mild exasperation, she wrote that her "good man" had "wished to remember so many at Christmas—that he kept Miss Patterson and I [*sic*] running to find what he wanted. I went to town three days with her—and finally she had to go again."

Like their counterparts elsewhere, Bloomington residents began stringing up simple, handmade Christmas decorations for the first time in the 1860s, but they hung the decorations in their local churches and not in the family parlor, as Sarah described in a letter to David (December 26, 1871): "In the evening Fanny and I went to a Festival for the Children of our Sabbath School given by the Ladies of the Church. I gave them evergreen from two small pieces of hedge that we wished to destroy and the Church was very prettily decorated. . . . The chandeliers were wreathed and the table filled with Cakes, handsomely iced—and three Pyramids of macaroons covered with a veil of spun candy set off the table handsomely—nuts, raisins, and candies . . . constituted the rest of the refreshments. . . . A large evergreen tree in the center of the church hung with popcorn strung and hung in festoons—and balls of corn candy wrapped in bright colored tissue paper attracted the children and was robbed by them at the close of the evening."

By the late 1870s, when she was living in her elegant, new mansion, Sarah was still celebrating Thanksgiving, but, like many of her contemporaries, she was beginning to shift her attention to Christmas. For one thing, she was now performing the same acts of charity at Christmas that she had reserved for Thanksgiving. She instructed her servants to prepare baskets of meats, baked goods, and staples to be delivered to needy families at both holidays. In addition, she served the same foods at Christmas that she had served at Thanksgiving: turkey, gravy, and cranberries, along with mince-meat pies, cookies, and candy.

Most importantly, she began talking for the very first time about decorating her home for the holidays. She instructed her husband to see if he could find some ever-greens on his way home from Washington, D.C., during the Christmas recess, because she wished to festoon these new fashions around her home. On December 3, 1876, after giving David explicit instructions about the kinds of evergreens she wanted, she confided: "I like the custom of decorating the rooms at Christmas. . . ."

We will never know whether Sarah Davis would eventually have embraced Christmas with the same devotion that she felt for Thanksgiving. While visiting family in Massachusetts in 1879, Sarah died suddenly after a brief illness, just as she was becoming interested in the Victorians' newly invented Christmas customs. Nonetheless, she left behind a beautiful home, where her children could begin celebrating the elaborate kind of Christmas that she may never have envisioned.

As a reminder of that late-Victorian celebration, the Davis Mansion exhibits a special kind of candy on the dining table every Christmas because Victorians loved candy! Their cookbooks were filled with recipes for all kinds of sweets—everything from taffy and cotton (spun) candy to chocolate and caramels. Since Christmas was now considered a home-based holiday focused upon children's needs, it was considered the ideal time for confectioners to show off their skills. Each December they made a variety of candies out of caramelized sugar and chocolate, which they molded into shapes to make them seem real.

Some of the most realistic-looking shapes included sausages, boiled lobsters, and various animals, but Victorian children especially loved insect-shaped candies, such as beetles and spiders. Although nineteenth-century candy makers popularized a variety of insect-shaped confections, *chocolate-molded cockroaches* were a special favorite!

Sarah Davis was familiar with the tradition of giving candy cockroaches and similar sweets during the Christmas season. Across the street from Sarah's home (while she was growing up in Lenox, Massachusetts) lived the Sedgwick family, whose daughter, Kate, received the following letter (dated January 1831) from a cousin in New York City: "When we were all dressed, we prepared to go into Mama's room to get our New Year's presents. . . . I took out a box and opened it and found some sugar-men, some candy, a cockroach-sugar also and some cherries (sugar!)." Each year, to keep this New-England-based, Victorian tradition alive, the Davis Mansion decorates the dining table with chocolate cockroaches and serves samples to visitors touring the home at Christmastime.

A Christmas Eve Fight

NEW YORK TIMES

Even after the Civil War and peaceful family Christmases became the norm in Illinois, Christmas celebrations could still become boisterous. The New York Times *saw fit to place this story of a Christmas dust-up in Shawneetown on page one of its December 26, 1889, edition.*

A free fight took place at a Christmas celebration in Eagle Creek Precinct last night, at which chairs, clubs, knives, and pistols were used. Thomas Burroughs, the church doorkeeper, and one of the most respectable and prominent farmers in the county, was dangerously stabbed in two places; Stout Colbert was hit in the chin with a bullet, and several other persons received minor injuries.

The fight arose from a mistake in distributing the presents. As is usual at such entertainments, parents in the neighborhood had taken their gifts to the church, where they were properly labeled and hung up on the tree. Some of the tags were insecurely fastened and dropped off, but were replaced as accurately as possible. Last night a large crowd assembled to witness the distribution. When about a dozen of the presents had been handed to the children, a farmer named Johnson grabbed a sled from a child's hands and declared that it was one he had brought there for his little boy. The sexton attempted to explain his mistake, but Johnson pushed him rudely aside and started for the door, carrying the sled in his hands. Some young men who had been drinking tried to snatch the sled from Johnson, and he struck one of them, and was himself hit with a chair and felled to the floor. The fight then became general, and for a time it looked as though a number of the combatants would be killed.

After Christmas

CHAMPAIGN COUNTY GAZETTE

By the end of Queen Victoria's reign, Christmas came to be valued for its tranquillity and civility. At least this seemed to be the case during this 1898 Christmas in Champaign.

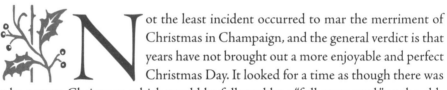 **N**ot the least incident occurred to mar the merriment of Christmas in Champaign, and the general verdict is that years have not brought out a more enjoyable and perfect Christmas Day. It looked for a time as though there was to be a green Christmas, which would be followed by a "full grave yard," as the old-timers say, but when Santa Claus had completed his mission and was speeding away, there came in his tracks a snow storm from the north. It was one of those good old snow storms which add so much to the Christmas cheer, and when children, and grown people, too, looked from the window Sunday morning, they were delighted, for snow adds everything to Christmastime.

As was outlined in the *Gazette* Friday evening, there were Christmas entertainments in a majority of the churches of the city Saturday evening. Children were out by the hundreds, they listened to and took part in the Christmas songs and recitations, and each of them went back home carrying a small bag of fruit, nuts, and candy. In all the churches the entertainments moved off with perfect regularity, there was not so

J. P. McCollum home, Champaign, 1950

much as a small fire or an accident of any character to mar the pleasures of the occasion, and old Santa Claus never appeared in better humor and spirits.

The customary Christmas quiet prevailed Sunday. The whole city was up unusually early, for everybody had to see what Santa Claus had brought, and the remainder of the day was devoted to trying on neckties, playing with jumping jacks, and eating turkey. In all the churches there were special Christmas services, and they were without an exception well attended. When night settled over the city the inhabitants, both old and young, were tired out and willing to retire without much effort.

Monday being the legal holiday, it was accepted by the business people of the city, and while some of the business houses remained open all day, they might as well have closed early in the morning and remained closed, for there was no business of any character, and the business portion of the city took on the aspect of a genuine Sunday. Only people who were compelled to, were downtown, leaving the streets practically deserted during the afternoon.

The desk reports at the police station Tuesday showed that men addicted to strong drink had gone about their habit with moderation through respect for the good day, and only one man was hauled in during the day on the charge of intoxication. His Christmas present was one of unusual size; unfortunately he could not handle it and he had to pay three dollars and costs for the privilege of getting someone else to handle it.

All told, it was a Christmas holiday which made the people feel happy and glad that they were alive and nothing more could have been expected of it. When it did this it had fulfilled its mission.

I Came a Stranger

HILDA SATT POLACHECK

Jane Addams's Hull-House spawned pleasurable memories for many immigrants seeking to be accepted in their new country. For Hilda Satt Polacheck, her first Christmas at Hull-House became indelible.

everal days before Christmas 1896, one of my Irish playmates suggested that I go with her to a Christmas party at Hull-House. I told her that I never went to Christmas parties.

"Why not?" she asked.

"I do not go anywhere on Christmas Day," I said.

"But this party will not be on Christmas Day. It will be the Sunday before Christmas Day," she said.

I repeated that I could not go and she persisted in wanting to know why. Before I could think, I blurted out the words: "I might get killed."

"Get killed!" She stared at me. "I go to Hull-House Christmas parties every year, and no one was ever killed."

I then asked her if there would be any Jewish children at the party. She assured me that there had been Jewish children at the parties every year and that no one was ever hurt.

The thought began to percolate through my head that things might be different in America. In Poland it had not been safe for Jewish children to be on the streets on Christmas. I struggled with my conscience and finally decided to accompany my friend to the Hull-House Christmas party. This was the second time I was doing something without telling Mother.

My friend and I arrived at Hull-House and went to the coffee shop where the party was being held. There were many children and their parents seated when we arrived. It was the first time that I had sat in a room where there was a Christmas tree. In fact, there were two trees in the room: one on each side of the high brick fireplace. The trees looked as if they had just been brought in from a heavy snowstorm. The glistening glass icicles and asbestos snow looked very real. The trees were lighted with white candles and on each side stood a man with a pail of water and a mop, ready to put out any accidental fire.

People called to each other across the room. Then I noticed that I could not understand what they were saying. It dawned on me that people in this room had come from other countries. Yet there was no tension. Everybody seemed to be having a good time. There were children and parents at this party from Russia, Poland, Italy, Germany, Ireland, England, and many other lands, but no one seemed to care where they had come from, or what religion they professed, or what clothes they wore, or what they thought. As I sat there, I am sure I felt myself being freed from a variety of century-old superstitions and inhibitions. There seemed to be nothing to be afraid of.

Then Jane Addams came into the room! It was the first time that I looked into those kind, understanding eyes. There was a gleam of welcome in them that made me feel I was wanted. She told us that she was glad we had come. Her voice was warm and I knew she meant what she said. [. . .]

The children of the Hull-House Music School then sang some songs, that I later found out were called "Christmas carols." I shall never forget the caressing sweetness of those childish voices. All feelings of religious intolerance and bigotry faded. I could not connect this beautiful party with any hatred or superstition that existed among the people of Poland.

As I look back, I know that I became a staunch American at this party. I was with children who had been brought here from all over the world. The fathers and mothers, like my father and mother, had come in search of a free and happy life. And we were all having a good time at a party, as the guests of an American, Jane Addams.

We were all poor. Some of us were underfed. Some of us had holes in our shoes. But we were not afraid of each other. What greater service can a human being give to her country than to banish fear from the heart of a child? Jane Addams did that for me at that party.

While I felt that I had done nothing wrong or sinful by going to the Christmas party, I still hesitated telling Mother where I had been. I was glad she did not ask me.

Black Christmas 1951

JACK McREYNOLDS

The trauma of community disasters, such as that of the Orient Number Two mine explosion on December 21, 1951, lingers for generations in the consciousness of those who experienced them. Each Christmas, Jack McReynolds, a teenager at the time of the event and later a career coal miner himself, remembers the disaster that directly affected families from throughout southern Illinois.

My thoughts go back sometimes as the holiday season approaches to a Christmas in my youth in the year of 1951. Mother had the tree up, as did most of our neighbors, and all of our thoughts were of the oncoming day of Christmas. I was a sophomore in high school in West Frankfort. I was sixteen years old at the time. Most of the kids in my school were also excited about the holidays. We would get out of school for about two weeks during this holiday season.

Friday evening, December 21, our high school basketball team was playing Marion at our new gym. I attended the game as did many others. The game started at 7:00 P.M. I forget who was winning at the time, but at about 7:30, time out was called, and the announcer said, "Would Dr. Lambert please report to the Number Four New Orient Mine portal." A few people started milling around asking questions and talking among themselves. We all knew Dr. Lambert was the coal-company doctor, so this meant that there was someone hurt in the mine. The game resumed, and about fifteen minutes later, time out was called again. The announcer said, "Would any medical personnel and any more doctors and nurses please report to New Orient Portal Number Four."

Also, "Any funeral directors please go to Portal Number Four."

People knew something was very bad wrong at the mine. Then, before time out was over and the game resumed, approximately five minutes later, the announcer said, "Would any experienced coal miners please report to the New Orient Portal Number Four." People started leaving the gym in numbers then, all knowing something was terribly wrong at the mine. I was told later that over seven hundred people left the gym that evening.

Our Christmas
Disaster, *1952*
*(cover drawing by
Robert Youngman)*

I and three of my friends also left, being curious as sixteen-year-olds are, and got into an old 1936 Ford car and drove out to the mine portal. The portal was located about four miles northwest of town, and when we arrived, police had the road to the portal blocked, so we parked the car and climbed over a fence and walked about a quarter of a mile to the portal. Smoke was boiling out of the mouth of the mine like a chimney. I remember looking up at the tipple and watching pigeons that normally roosted up there at night just falling over and dropping down the shaft from being overcome with carbon monoxide. It was maybe an hour or two when the men who went below started bringing bodies up on the cage and carrying them on stretchers into the wash house. Finally, I think maybe it was the police or mine personnel told us to leave, and we went home shocked at what we had seen. My mother had already heard the news from another neighbor I assume.

She was sitting at the kitchen table crying, because she had relatives at the mine and many friends who worked there. I remember the next morning when we got up, which was Saturday morning, Mom was taking the Christmas tree down and trying to explain to me that there was not anything to be joyful about this year with so many men perished, and maybe trapped somewhere in the mine. I went to my friend's house, and his mother was taking her tree down also. And most people we knew where doing the same thing.

I remember my Aunt Grace Ramsey being there and telling Mom that her husband, Uncle Dick Ramsey, was at the mine helping retrieve any survivors, and also bringing bodies out. His brother, Alex Ramsey, was one of the dead. A boyhood friend of mine, Billy McDaniels, was among the dead. He was just eighteen and had just started working there a couple of months beforehand.

As days passed and hopes of any survivors went away, there came a glimmer of hope. The news was, "A miner was found alive after four days." The man's name was Cecil Sanders. I think he was from the Benton area. But that was the only one who survived. Many of my classmates lost their fathers or brothers, uncles and friends that terrible evening.

I remember going to the Heights Cemetery and looking at twelve or fifteen open graves waiting on the funerals. There were about twenty funerals on Christmas Eve, and maybe that many on Christmas Day. I also remember being at the junior high school gym, which was being used as a morgue, and seeing many, many bodies lying on the gym floor and many people coming in and identifying their loved ones if possible and hearing the cries of anguish when finding a loved one among the dead. It was the most horrible thing I had ever seen.

In later years when I started my career in the coal mines, if I was working on December 21, I would always say to my fellow miners, "Boys, this is the day Orient Number Two blew up. Let's be extra careful today!" I went ahead and worked almost thirty-five years underground and saw men killed down in the mine in accidents, have been in a few mine fires and in one explosion myself and had to walk out the escape way, and such. But none ever compared with the night Orient Number Two mine blew up, and we all lost 119 of our relatives and friends and neighbors. There was hardly a family in town and the surrounding towns who didn't know someone who was killed there.

There were black wreaths hanging on many front doors that Christmas. But each and every year on December 21, I always remember that terrible night. I have never forgot that Christmas, and never will forget it!

Christmas in Chicago

ELOISE JORDAN

Eloise Jordan bases her account of Chicago Christmas celebrations on historical records. From homespun to commercial, the evolution of Chicago Christmas is not unlike that throughout the rest of the state.

When Fort Dearborn was young, the settlers of the little frontier hamlet at the mouth of the Chicago River had little more than the spirit of Christmas to enhance their holiday celebrations. But that spirit was the essential ingredient, and Christmas early-Chicago-style, in a setting that could be the model for all we mean by "a good old-fashioned Christmas," was warm, hearty, and hospitable.

Spruce and pine trees in dense shrubbery lined the shores on both sides of the river, and late in December a heavy blanket of snow covered the ground. Gazing toward Lake Michigan from the fort, over the level white expanse, the land, frozen river, and the lake seemed one smooth unbroken prairie. One of the early records assures us that the air was pure and bracing.

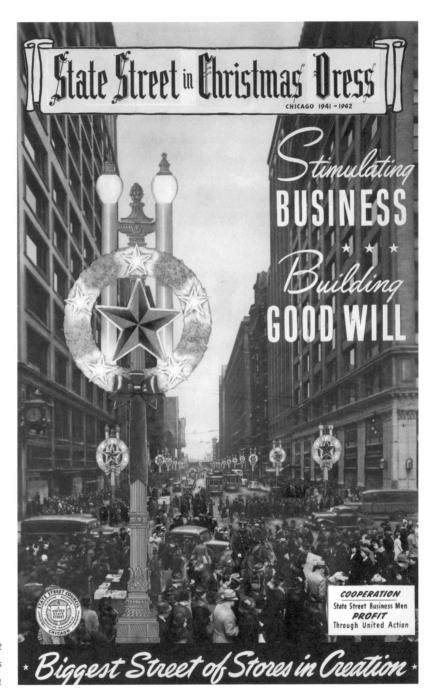

State Street
in Christmas
Dress, 1941

Cratchets' Christmas Dinner, Slotkowski Sausage Co. float, 1968

Angels on float in front of the Chicago Theater, 1956

The cabins, sparsely located in clearings in the wilderness under the protective shadow of the sturdy new fort, were inhabited by families of French or American settlers. Indians of the region, drawn by opportunities for trade or barter, were frequent visitors. The principal contacts with the outside world were the traders who came through bringing news and wares to the garrison and the civilians of the settlement. Most of the settlers undoubtedly celebrated Christmas inside the fort with the soldiers and their families.

The limitations of frontier life, and the lack of shops, did not deter joyful, bustling preparations for this holiday. Emphasis was on the Christmas dinner and on the gay visits with one another. Everything eaten was hard-earned. The soldiers and trappers brought in turkeys from the forest which also provided venison, quail, wild duck, and prairie chicken. And the women pooled their meager supplies to make the traditional Christmas dessert, plum pudding topped with flaming brandy. When dinner was announced by the beat of a drum, it was approached by a grateful people.

The entertainment after dinner, self-provided, continued the merriment. The family of John Kinzie, a successful early trader who lived in a cabin on the north bank across the river from the fort, would be among the guests. Kinzie, a skillful fiddler, accompanied by fife and drums, played the tunes for the dancers.

Here, then, was one of Chicago's first Christmases, without modern trappings, but with a real community celebration, gay with the warmth and spirit which symbolize the true meaning of the day.

By 1840, Christmas in Chicago had become more of a family holiday. The scattered cabins of the earlier period were no orderly rows of houses. Churches had been built, local government was in the hands of elected officials, and news of the world was supplied by Chicago's first newspapers. During the holiday season, religious services made up the more serious side of observances. Christmas dinner was still the high point of the social festivities. Skating and sleighing on the river in straw-filled cutters were gay aftermaths. Some of the more sports-minded might arrange a horse race on the ice, or, even more exciting, hunt the wolves that occasionally roamed into the town. There were few gifts, but there was much fun and good fellowship.

It was in 1838 that a really gala Christmas celebration was held at the newly built Lake Hotel, one of the first brick buildings in Chicago. This was an invitation affair, a nicety the proprietor, a Connecticut Yankee, brought with him from the east. Sixty years later, Fernando Jones, for many years Chicago's oldest inhabitant, in a reminiscent mood vividly recalled this occasion with its French cookery, bills-of-fare, toothpicks, and other newfangled ideas.

Christmas in Chicago after the Fire of October 9, 1871, was understandably more subdued than in previous years. Compared to 1840, the city had undergone remarkable growth in area, population, and in the scope of social activities. This season, however, shoppers had to depend on makeshift stores, limited stocks of Christmas toys, candy, and household goods. Gifts, in general, were less expensive and of a utilitarian nature, for the Fire had wiped out the businesses, homes, and possessions of more than ninety-five thousand Chicagoans, one-third of the population. Boxes of goods and toys had been distributed to the homeless by the Relief and Aid Society, and clothing from all over the country arrived for the many needy.

At the same time, it is interesting to note the Christmas items advertised by the merchants: mink, ermine, and seal furs for the ladies; jewelry; boots and shoes; crockery; fashionable millinery; stereoscopic and photographic views of Chicago before and after the Fire; books; and of all things, canaries!

For this Christmas, little more than ten weeks after the Fire, Chicagoans bought such foods as they could and enjoyed such amusement as they could afford. As in the past, they attended church services, visited friends, and skated in the parks. The theater season was very much alive, what with matinee or evening performances to choose from in at least three theaters. "The Mistletoe Bough" was playing at the Globe, "Caste" at the Michigan Avenue Theater, and minstrels held forth at the West Side Opera House—all three theaters playing to full houses.

Happily, the festive Christmas spirit was not burned out by the Fire. The ashes were hardly cool before Chicagoans were busy rebuilding their city and resuming their accustomed social activities. Indeed, the Fire seemed to be a turning point in the life of the city and its incredible development afterward.

The story of the Christmas Tree Ship is a unique part of Chicago Christmas lore. It started one day in early December 1887, when a two-masted schooner made its way up the Chicago River and docked at the old Clark Street bridge. She had come from northern Michigan and was deep-laden with a fragrant cargo of green, snow-powdered Christmas trees. Jolly, likeable Herman Schuenemann was captain of the ship. He and his younger brother, August, had gone into the woods near Manistique, Michigan, to cut spruces, pines, and balsams for the Chicago market.

Living was unpretentious and money was not too plentiful in Chicago sixty-eight years ago, but Christmas was a friendly, neighborly holiday most often celebrated at home. Chicagoans were captivated with the idea of picking out a tree from the heaps of evergreens aboard the Schuenemann schooner under a sign which read: "The Christmas Tree Ship. My Prices Are the Lowest." The trees sold so well, and the affable brothers made so many friends, that year after year they returned. The Christmas season did not really begin until the Christmas Tree Ship tied up here.

In 1898, August Schuenemann was lost with his ship when it floundered in a storm. The Christmas Tree Ship did not call at Chicago that year, but the next year and for many years after, Captain Herman brought in his load of trees on the *Rouse Simmons*, his newly acquired three-masted schooner. Late in November 1912, in threatening weather, the *Rouse Simmons* cleared for Chicago carrying a deckload of fifty thousand trees. Snow was falling, and a pounding gale swept out of the northwest. Coast Guardsmen reported seeing her, sails tattered, coated in ice, deck bare, and distress signals flying—then she vanished into the blinding storm. That was the last seen of the *Rouse Simmons*, her captain and crew; but for months after, the nets of fishermen on the Wisconsin side of the lake were entangled with Christmas trees.

1931 - 1932

Greetings from Thornhill, the Morton Arboretum, 1931

CHRISTMAS IN ILLINOIS HISTORY ✦ ✦ ✦ ✦ ✦ ✦ ✦ ✦ ✦ ✦ ✦ ✦ ✦ ✦ ✦ ✦ ✦ ✦

The Schuenemann family carried on the business for years, and when they gave it up, the Christmas Tree Ship became a cherished memory to add to the store of past joyous Christmas seasons in Chicago.

On the surface it might seem that Christmas in Chicago today is a far cry, indeed, from the homespun holiday celebrations of earlier days. Our Christmas-season observances are now characterized by miles of gaily decorated streets, stores filled with holiday merchandise, window displays which are the fruit of months of planning, lavishly trimmed community and family Christmas trees, and a variety of charitable works.

While the scope of our festivities is vastly increased, the traditional meanings and forms are preserved in our holiday music, art, and literature. It is the same Christmas spirit of the humble Fort Dearborn days, of the convivial 1830s, and of Chicago after the Fire which underlies all our holiday activities. Christmas celebrations in Chicago are variations on an old theme which has been and still is MERRY CHRISTMAS!

Julbock and Tomten,
Bishop Hill, by
Mike Wendel

Living Traditions

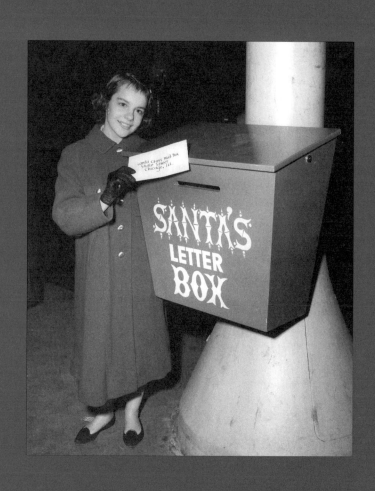

Dear Santa

Before sitting on Santa's lap in department stores became the way children let Santa and their parents know what they wanted for Christmas, letter writing was common, and often post-office employees volunteered to answer the letters that might otherwise have wound up in the dead letter file. Today many children e-mail Santa. These handwritten letters to Santa from children of Vermilion County were printed in the Fairmount Review, December 6, 1909.

Dear Santa,
I would like a football and a game of fishpond, a bugle horn, and a drum. If it is not too much, bring a tool chest, a little ship, some nuts and oranges.

Goodwin Maxfield

Dear Santa,
I have tried to be a good boy all summer. For Christmas I thought it was time to write now. I want an air gun and an overcoat, of course I like candy and oranges and nuts. I think it is time to close. My stocking will be on the chair.

Your friend,
Dale Delaney

*Facing page:
Santa's letter
box, 1958*

Dear Santa,

I am seven years old. I wish you would bring me a doll with pretty black hair and some doll clothes and bed and dresser, this is all, for you have so many to give to, only don't forget my cousin Goldie. She is bad sick.

Thelma Snow

Dear Santa Claus,

I will tell you what I would like to have. I want a tablet, a pencil and pencil box; but if you have anything else for me you can bring it.

Grace L. Britt

Dear Santa Claus,

I am a little farmer boy, and I want for Christmas: a horn, a sweater, a rocking horse and a story book and a pair of mittens. I want lots of fruit, candy and nuts. That is all for this time.

Your little friend,
Edward Cheuvront

Dear Santa Claus,

I am a little boy three years old. I have been real good and would like for you to bring me a box of blocks, a little drum, a wagon, doll, a new overcoat and some peanuts and candy.

Your little boy,
Paul Steenbergen

Dear Santa Claus,

I have been a good girl and go to school every day. I would like to get a doll dresser, a ring and a pair of rubbers to keep my shoes clean. Helen wants a doll, a teddy bear and a purse. Don't forget the fruit and nuts. Dear Santa, this is all for today so I will close, hoping to see you at our school house for we are going to have a Christmas tree.

Good-bye from
Theresa Hart

Dear Santa Claus,

I have been sick ever since the thirteenth of August and am partly crippled yet. If you have any presents for me please bring them. I will be glad of anything you bring.

Bernie Robert Britt

What I Want for Christmas

ROBERT GREEN INGERSOLL

Adults have also used the holiday to make known to others their desires for the future. Robert Green Ingersoll, the son of a Presbyterian abolitionist minister, taught in Mount Vernon and Metropolis and practiced law in Shawneetown and Peoria. He was a colonel in the Union army and after the war became Illinois attorney general before becoming prominent on the national stage. In his "Christmas Sermon," written in 1892, he said, "I believe in Christmas and in every day that has been set aside for joy." The following requests for Christmas, written in 1897, express his humanism.

If I had the power to produce exactly what I want for next Christmas, I would have all the kings and emperors resign and allow the people to govern themselves.

I would have all the nobility crop their titles and give their lands back to the people. I would have the pope throw away his tiara, take off his sacred vestments, and admit that he is not acting for God—is not infallible—but is just an ordinary Italian. I would have all the cardinals, archbishops, bishops, priests, and clergymen admit that they know nothing about theology, nothing about hell or heaven, nothing about the destiny of the human race, nothing about devils or ghosts, gods or angels. I would have them tell all their "flocks" to think for themselves, to be manly men and womanly women, and to do all in their power to increase the sum of human happiness.

I would have all the professors in colleges, all the teachers in schools of every kind, including those in Sunday schools, agree that they would teach only what they know, that they would not palm off guesses as demonstrated truths.

I would like to see all the politicians changed to statesmen—to men who long to make their country great and free; to men who care more for public good than private gain—men who long to be of use.

I would like to see all the editors of papers and magazines agree to print the truth and nothing but the truth, to avoid all slander and misrepresentation, and to let the private affairs of the people alone.

I would like to see drunkenness and prohibition both abolished.

I would like to see corporal punishment done away with in every home, in every school, in every asylum, reformatory, and prison. Cruelty hardens and degrades; kindness reforms and ennobles.

I would like to see the millionaires unite and form a trust for the public good.

I would like to see a fair division of profits between capital and labor, so that the toiler could save enough to mingle a little June with the December of his life.

I would like to see an international court established in which to settle disputes between nations, so that armies could be disbanded and the great navies allowed to rust and rot in perfect peace.

I would like to see the whole world free—free from injustice—free from superstition.

This will do for next Christmas. The following Christmas, I may want more.

An Echo of Old Christmas

JOHN W. ALLEN

Christmas celebrations from European cultures are still practiced throughout Illinois. Prairie du Rocher and Teutopolis have two of the longest traditions.

Those who came from foreign lands and from other sections of our own country to make their homes in southern Illinois often brought with them their customs and their lore. One practice that came with the early French settlers was *La Guiannée*, a jolly greeting given at each New Year at Prairie du Rocher in Randolph County. A second, from Germany this time, was Old Christmas with its "Three Kings" song. This is celebrated each January 6 in the Teutopolis region of Effingham County.

Each of these, really observed on the eve of the day honored, has its centuries-old history. And each is as firmly established in Illinois. Neither has been modernized, and thus both remain distinctly folk practices. *La Guiannée* came to the Kaskaskia-Cahokia region with the French in the early 1700s. Three Kings, already a feature of Old Christmas in Germany, began to be formally observed in Illinois shortly after the concentrated German-Catholic settlement was begun near Teutopolis.

Its present dramatized version was started here by Benjamin Voss, who came directly from Germany to Illinois considerably more than a hundred years ago. The door-to-door visit of the Three Kings immediately became the most prominent feature of the Old Christmas observance among the German settlers. Both the German text and the English translation are credited to Voss.

The song is a narrative poem that tells the journey of the Three Wise Men. One of these was Melchior, the smallish King of Nubia, who came bearing gifts of gold to represent wealth. With him came Balthasar, the middle-sized King of Chaldea, whose gift was frankincense, which is burned for its pleasing odor and was considered emblematic of the common man. Gaspar, the King of Tarsus, or Tarshia, the largest and most impressive of the three in stature, brought myrrh, used in incense and in perfume. It was considered emblematic of man's humility.

During the enactment at Teutopolis a strong staff to represent divine support and strength is carried by Balthasar. Gaspar carries a broom to sweep away all trouble and misfortune. All are impressively robed and bedecked for the occasion. Their robes, made by local women, are carefully laundered after each use and made ready for the next appearance.

Though the Teutopolis area is about as concentratedly Catholic a community as one finds in America, calls made by the singers and their accordionist are not restricted to Catholic homes. The Lutheran minister invites and welcomes them, as do others.

As the place of call—a home, a hospital, the priest's house, the Sisters' home, the lodging of the infirm, or even a tavern—is approached, the accordion strikes up the air of the song. Someone opens the door and welcomes the troupe. One looking on at any place of call notes a respectful silence, even in a tavern, when the musicians enter. It is indeed a strange feeling one has in a tavern, where the walls are decorated with beer signs, pictures of pin-up girls, hunting scenes, arty calendars, pictures of sports events, and noted athletes. But somehow all of these seem to fade into the background and become insignificant. Each singer in turn announces the name of the king he represents. The seated musician starts playing, and the song is begun.

Where children are present the general expression of awe is evident. The middle-aged give relaxed attention. On older faces one sees a look of wistful remembering. Many an oldster will be seen making almost imperceptible lip movements in rhythm with the music, as if to form the words. Occasionally, a less restrained older person may audibly join in the song. In one case, so many did this that it became a chorus.

The "Three Kings" song tells of the Wise Men's journey of thirteen days in which they traveled four hundred miles. It tells of the star that guided them until it had stopped over the crib of the infant Jesus. To represent this guiding star, a staff with a rotating star mounted on it is carried by one of the kings in the enactment. At the manger its rotation is stopped, and it rests just as the guiding star did above the place where the Christ child lay. Its stopping represents the end of their long journey.

The robed singers then kneel and extend their hands as if to present the gifts they have brought. After a slight pause, the remaining portion of the song that extends greetings of the season and invokes blessings is sung, and a calm happiness seems to settle on the gathering.

The song is very old. The earliest record found indicates its use in Germany in 1072. Later records and references show increased observances. "Three Kings" is sung in German, just as *La Guiannée* is sung in French. This often baffles outsiders and the youngsters who are only casually acquainted with those languages.

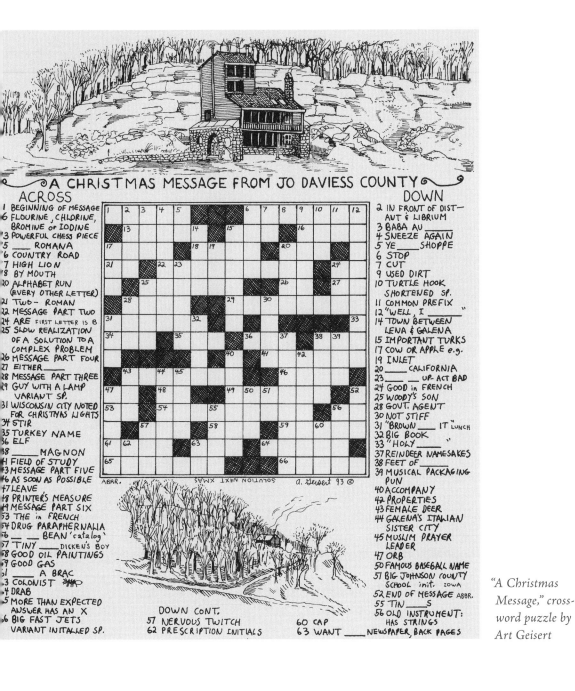

A CHRISTMAS MESSAGE FROM JO DAVIESS COUNTY

ACROSS

1 BEGINNING OF MESSAGE
6 FLOURINE, CHLORINE, BROMINE or IODINE
13 POWERFUL CHESS PIECE
15 ____ ROMANA
16 COUNTRY ROAD
17 HIGH LION
18 BY MOUTH
20 ALPHABET RUN (EVERY OTHER LETTER)
21 TWO-ROMAN
22 MESSAGE PART TWO
24 ARE FIRST LETTER IS B
25 SLOW REALIZATION OF A SOLUTION TO A COMPLEX PROBLEM
26 MESSAGE PART FOUR
27 EITHER ____
28 MESSAGE PART THREE
29 GUY WITH A LAMP VARIANT SP.
31 WISCONSIN CITY NOTED FOR CHRISTMAS LIGHTS
34 STIR
35 TURKEY NAME
36 ELF
38 ____ MAGNON
41 FIELD OF STUDY
43 MESSAGE PART FIVE
46 AS SOON AS POSSIBLE
47 LEAVE
48 PRINTER'S MEASURE
49 MESSAGE PART SIX
53 THE in FRENCH
54 DRUG PARAPHERNALIA
56 ____ BEAN 'catalog'
57 TINY ____ DICKEN'S BOY
58 GOOD OIL PAINTINGS
59 GOOD GAS
61 ____ A BRAC
63 COLONIST
64 DRAB
65 MORE THAN EXPECTED ANSWER HAS AN X
66 BIG FAST JETS VARIANT IN TALLED SP.

DOWN

2 IN FRONT OF DIST-AUT & LIBRIUM
3 BABA AU ____
4 SNEEZE AGAIN
5 YE ____ SHOPPE
6 STOP
7 CUT
9 USED DIRT
10 TURTLE HOOK SHORTENED SP.
11 COMMON PREFIX
12 "WELL, I ____"
14 TOWN BETWEEN LENA & GALENA
15 IMPORTANT TURKS
17 COW OR APPLE e.g.
19 INLET
20 ____ CALIFORNIA
23 ____ UP ACT BAD
24 GOOD in FRENCH
25 WOODY'S SON
28 GOVT. AGENT
30 NOT STIFF
31 "BROWN ____ IT" LUNCH
32 BIG BOOK
33 "HOLY ____"
37 REINDEER NAMESAKES
38 FEET OF ____
39 MUSICAL PACKAGING PUN
40 ACCOMPANY
42 PROPERTIES
43 FEMALE DEER
44 GALENA'S ITALIAN SISTER CITY
45 MUSLIM PRAYER LEADER
47 ORB
50 FAMOUS BASEBALL NAME
51 BIG JOHNSON COUNTY SCHOOL init. IOWA
52 END OF MESSAGE ABBR.
55 TIN ____ S
56 OLD INSTRUMENT: HAS STRINGS

DOWN CONT.

57 NERVOUS TWITCH
62 PRESCRIPTION INITIALS
60 CAP
63 WANT ____ NEWSPAPER, BACK PAGES

ABBR.

SOLUTION NEXT XMAS

a. Geisert 93 ©

"A Christmas Message," crossword puzzle by Art Geisert

Julotta Services Here to Draw
Ten Thousand Worshipers

ROCKFORD REGISTER STAR

Swedish communities throughout Illinois have celebrated the Julotta (early Christmas-morning service). Both Julotta and the celebration of Santa Lucia mark the holidays for Swedish Americans and many others who are drawn to the events surrounding them. This 1950 story describes a century of such celebrations in Rockford.

"Julotta" is a word full of meaning and sentiment in Rockford. It is the name of the Christmas matin service before the break of day which remains a tradition in many Rockford churches even though they have dropped the Swedish language and in some instances have never used it. It has always been the best-attended service of the year and it still continues to maintain that status in most churches here.

The Julotta was brought to Rockford by the first Swedish settlers when they came here in 1852. It is not known if their first worship service in a residence Christmas Day, 1853, was a Julotta, but it seems quite certain that from 1855, when they had completed the basement of their first church building, the Julotta has been a dominant part of the Christmas observance in Rockford. It is probable they had a Julotta in an unused school house in 1854.

Fifteen more Rockford churches will attract ten thousand or more worshipers Christmas morning to Julottas which will begin in some churches as early as 5:30 A.M. and in others as late as 6:30 A.M. Most of them begin at 6:00 A.M.

In the old days, Julottas usually began at 5:00 A.M. and it was not uncommon that worshipers would begin arriving as early as 3:00 A.M. to get choice seats in the churches, which usually were well filled by 4:00 A.M.

Julottas since 1855

First Lutheran church, which was organized by the Swedish newcomers on January 15, 1854, has the longest tradition of Julotta services in Rockford. Its first one was held in the basement of their first incompleted church at North First Street and the old Rock Street, Christmas morning, 1855. It was a still more joyous Julotta the following year, Christmas 1856, because by then the church building was completed. It had been dedicated on November 23 of that year by Dr. T. N. Hasselquist, who described the church as the finest that had been built in this country by the Swedish newcomers up to that time. It was not a pretentious building, but it appeared so to the Swedish worshipers. It had been built at a cost of $775, for which the architect's fee was three dollars. It was forty-five feet long, twenty-eight feet wide, and sixteen feet high. The congregation also had its first pastor, the Rev. Andreas Andreen, who had just arrived in August 1856.

By Christmas 1857, the First Lutheran church congregation had purchased its first little reed organ for eighty-five dollars. It is made of rosewood and resembles a melodeon with lyre ends. It has two metal pedals, much like the present-day piano pedals, and three octave keys.

It took the young congregation a year and a half to pay for it. It has been saved by the congregation.

Axel Farb, 1602 South Fifth Street, who celebrated his eighty-sixth birthday December 3, recalled Saturday that he attended the first Julotta service in the present First Lutheran church building at South Third and Oak Streets on Christmas 1884. He has attended a great many Julottas in that church since that first time.

He recalled he had come from Sweden in 1883 and that Christmas attended Julotta in Alta, Iowa. By 1884, he was living with a cousin at Wesley corners on Montague Road near Rockford.

Traveled by Bobsled

"We went to church with a bobsled but it was so cold that we ran after the sled instead of riding in it," Farb said yesterday. The Rev. Gustaf Peters was pastor and preached the Julotta service.

"We left the farm house about 2:00 A.M.," Farb recalled. "We just didn't go to bed at all." He recalled that it was the farmers who usually got to the church first.

Mr. Farb also recalled the first Julotta he attended when a child only three or four years old in Sweden. "I was so young that my father carried me," Farb said, "but it is a Julotta I shall never forget. When I saw the pastor flailing his arms as he preached seriously, I became scared and hid under my father's long coat. I thought the pastor was angry and I told my mother afterward that 'if he had come out of his box [pulpit] we could have had an unhappy encounter.' I also froze my ears on that trip to and from church and I made up my mind never to go to church any more."

Farb said he later changed his mind and that Julottas, except for the first one, have many pleasant memories for him. His first Julotta, he recalled, was in Lommaryd church about twenty-five miles from Jonkoping.

Worshipers Arrived Early

There are probably quite a few older members of First church who can recall attending the first Julotta service in the present church building. It is the third church building of the congregation, and although it was built in 1883–84 it is still the largest church auditorium in Rockford. Farb said that the large church auditorium was always filled at Julotta with worshipers, who arrived about 4:00 A.M.

Many in the early days did as they had done in Sweden. They carried lighted torches, or "bloss," mostly of lighted pine knots. Arriving at the church, these torches were thrown in a pile in front of the church and there formed a cheery fire, around which the early comers would warm themselves before entering the church.

Everybody felt it necessary to attend Julotta. Many came from the country by horse and sleigh. Some even walked miles and miles. Eva Greta Carlsdotter, later Mrs. John C. Brolin, a member of the First church confirmation class in 1857, lived in Pecatonica, but in spite of the distance, fourteen miles, she had her heart set on attending Julotta in her own church in Rockford.

Froze Feet en Route

Being young and strong, she started out Christmas Eve for Rockford afoot and alone. The weather turned extremely cold and the snow was deep, almost impassable in places. But Eva Greta in dogged determination plodded on and arrived at the church on North First Street some time ahead of the start of the service. Unfortunately, her feet were badly frozen and she had to get them thawed out in a home close by the church. This was the spirit that dominated the early Swedish pioneers who settled in Rockford.

The first Christmas celebration by the Swedish newcomers took place in 1853, when the majority of the new families gathered in the home of Jonas Larson and John Sparf. It is not reported if this was a Julotta service in the meaning of that word or not. The worshipers, having no pastor, read appropriate passages from the scriptures,

Santa Lucias,
Bishop Hill,
by Mike Wendel

sang their old Christmas hymns and songs, and exchanged presents. At the conclusion of the get-together, it is said that they were so moved by this spirit and probably by their loneliness that they embraced each other as tears flowed from their eyes. Jonas Larson, one of those present, in an interview in 1855, declared it was the most enjoyable and unforgettable gathering by the earliest Swedish settlers.

The room in which the celebration was held was decorated with evergreens and, as one of those present said, "we even had candles in the window."

In the early years, only one passenger bridge crossed Rock River at State Street. It was a covered wooden affair and women especially dreaded to use the bridge. Since many of the younger Swedish women were employed in homes on the west side, they made it a practice to cross the Rock River on the ice at Christmas time and throughout the winter months. Before the first church was built, church services were held in a disused one-room red brick schoolhouse facing south in what was then the east-side park, now called Haight Park.

Santa Parade Is One Hundred

BRIAN KLEEMAN

Peorians lay claim to having the oldest continuing Santa Claus parade in the country. After more than 120 years, the parade continues to draw large crowds and marks the beginning of the community's holiday celebration, as it did on its centennial, decribed here in 1987.

When she was six years old, Marie Purtscher watched her first Santa Claus parade in downtown Peoria. "I don't remember much about the little things of the parade—that was so long ago," said the eighty-five-year-old Peoria woman. "It wasn't a big to-do like it is now. But I do remember the horses . . . and Santa Claus."

In the late 1930s and early 1940s, her husband, Anthony, was grand marshal of the parade. Since he died in 1967, she has not been to a parade. But she does enjoy watching them on television and hopes to watch this year.

"I think it's great," she beamed. "It's so much more elaborate now. All my kids have gone—and my ten grandchildren and eleven great-grandchildren."

Although Macy's parade attracts more attention at Thanksgiving, the nation's oldest Santa Claus parade belongs to Peoria. And on November 27, [1987], it will wind its way through downtown for the one hundredth time.

The small, one-band procession created in 1888 to attract more shoppers downtown is now an annual tradition.

The faces have changed over the years. The procession once started at the former Rock Island Depot [. . .] when Santa arrived on a special train leased by Block and Kuhl department store. It ended with Santa climbing the fire escape of the store—now the Jefferson Bank building—to Toyland.

"It's not Macy's, but we're making it as exciting as possible for the community," said Carl Bunker, the convention bureau's director of membership and community activities. "It's a one-day event that's over pretty quickly, but the children will remember it for a long, long time."

First sponsored by the privately owned Schipper and Block department store, the parade is now the ward of the Peoria Convention and Visitors Bureau and several

LIVING TRADITIONS ✦

Santa Claus
Headquarters,
Peoria

Caterpillar and
Mother Goose,
Peoria

Santa Parade,
Main Street,
Peoria

volunteer committees, which are busy putting together this year's effort: "Christmas Is for Children." The new committee structure allows for greater community participation in the planning of the event, Bunker added.

To celebrate the centennial, grand marshal Teddy Ruxpin will lead one hundred units through Peoria, including fourteen central Illinois bands, thirty floats from area businesses, novelty units, horses, and Santa Claus.

All floats are being rebuilt for the occasion at a cost of approximately twenty thousand dollars, paid by float sponsors, he said. And Santa will receive a new float as well.

The lighting of the Courthouse Plaza decorations following the parade will receive a new twist this year.

The Christmas Tree at the Peoria Civic Center will be lit the afternoon of the parade. Afterward, Mayor Jim Maloof will lead a procession of carolers along a luminary path through Fulton Plaza to the Courthouse Plaza. Santa then will light the Courthouse decorations, which will be more noticeable at night than after the parade, Bunker said.

The convention bureau even contacted President Reagan to attend the oldest Santa Parade in the country. "We're still waiting for feedback from that office," Bunker said.

It's a far cry from when Santa Claus first paraded through Peoria's brick streets in 1888.

Back then, Santa would arrive alone in a coach drawn by horses and would travel up to the store, where he would reside in Toyland.

It was no major event. In fact, tracing the early history of the parade is difficult. The store didn't advertise the coming of the man in the red suit and newspapers didn't think enough of the parade to cover it.

Schipper and Block, a downtown dry goods store, did advertise, though, that they were the exclusive Santa Claus headquarters in Peoria. And for several years, no other department store advertised having Santa at their store.

That changed by 1909, when Santa made his appearance in several other department stores. In December of that year, Schipper and Block wrote this in their monthly newsletter to store employees:

> Every year, Merrie Kriss comes thundering into the Union Station on his special "Toytown Express" and is escorted to the store by Spencer's Band. Some years there are rival Santas, but every little boy and girl knows where the genuine patron saint of childhood is to be found.

Sometime during these early years, a tradition of bringing Santa to town on the afternoon of the day after Thanksgiving began. Santa arrived by train every year until 1968, when the parade route changed.

In 1914, Schipper and Block became Block and Kuhl, and the Big White Store was built at the corner of Fulton and Adams Streets. Through 1921, Santa was met at the Rock Island Depot by a band and a "squadron of Peoria's finest police," who would escort him to the store.

In 1923, though, Block and Kuhl officials decided to expand the event from a one-band show into a major event.

"For thirty-five years the entry of Santa into Peoria has been the most spectacular event of the year in the lives of the young people of central Illinois," read an advertisement on Thanksgiving Day. "This year . . . it will be the most important pre-Christmas celebration, as far as we can learn, held by any store in the entire United States."

Two heralds on Arabian horses led the procession that included twelve policemen, four floats, a clown, and Santa. One float—the Old Woman in a Shoe—still is used sixty-four years after it first rolled down Peoria streets.

The Cinderella float, added the next year, also continues to be used. Within four years, the parade grew to thirty entries. Since then, new floats have come and gone, mostly focusing on nursery rhyme themes—Humpty Dumpty, Mother Goose, Ride Away Horse.

During the 1930s, horses were used to draw the floats through the parade. But when icy parade days made crossing the railroad tracks treacherous, LeTourneau and Caterpillar tractors were used to pull floats along the route.

In 1952 and 1953, Block and Kuhl bought the first floats not made in their Peoria warehouses. O. C. Polston of Clinton, owner of Polston Paint and Wallpaper, created ten floats and twenty walking pieces for the parade, which he had not seen before.

"I saw the parade in New York and just copied that," said the now-retired Polston. "My wife sold the idea to Block and Kuhl's."

Polston rarely watches the parade on television now, although his 'Twas the Night before Christmas and Little Miss Muffet floats are still used.

By the end of the 1950s, more than 140 units took part in the parade. An unusual addition to the festivities was the firing of aerial bombs from the roof of Block and Kuhl's, announcing Santa's arrival. That continued through the mid-1960s. And WMBD-TV began their live telecast in 1958.

Major changes in the 1960s brought an end to several parade traditions.

In 1961, Carson Pirie Scott and Company took over Block and Kuhl, but that store continued sponsoring the parade until 1966. The Central Illinois Santa Claus Parade Inc., under the Peoria Area Chamber of Commerce, took over the parade after seventy-eight years of private sponsorship.

The next year, Santa would begin a new tradition by ending his route at the Courthouse Plaza, where he would light the Christmas decorations.

A catastrophe nearly brought the annual event to an end in 1976. That summer, vandals damaged all of the floats for the parade, which were taken from storage in the Expo Hall at Exposition Gardens and placed in a nearby field during the 1976 Heart of Illinois Fair.

More than fifteen thousand dollars was needed to repair and restore all of the floats. However, the community banded together by raising the money and donating time to repair the floats at the last minute.

Similar damage occurred when a hailstorm damaged several floats in 1980. Again, the community came to the rescue to put on the parade.

Having weathered those storms, America's oldest Santa Claus parade seems healthy and ready to begin its second century.

Belleville Celebrates Its Christmas Traditions

ROBERT CHARLES HOWARD

As the conductor of the Belleville Philharmonic Orchestra ad Chorale writes, Christmas is a community affair in Belleville and has many of the German traditions, particularly music, practiced by its earliest settlers.

Belleville was founded by German immigrants in 1814, when Illinois was still a territory and was one of the earliest Illinois communities to celebrate Christmas. Barbara Kern of the St. Clair County Historical Society relates an event that affirms the city's early celebration of Christmas: "The first Christmas tree was the inspiration of Gustave Koerner, a German immigrant, who in 1833, for want of an evergreen tree, decorated a sassafras tree on a farm in Shiloh Valley. The St. Clair County

Trolley in the Square, Belleville

Santa Claus House, Belleville

Historical Society carried on this tradition by decorating a sassafras tree branch with antique ornaments in the Landmark Emma Kunz house in Belleville."

Today, mindful of its Germanic heritage, Belleville at Christmas teems with the sights and sounds of the season, celebrations enhanced by technology but suffused with echoes of the past. The town square and memorial fountain are adorned with Christmas trees, statues of carolers bundled up in nineteenth-century attire, and a Nativity scene. There are the sounds of hooves as a horse-drawn carriage passes by, while Christmas carols ring out from speakers placed on the gaslight lampposts hidden by holiday roping, snowflakes, and snowmen. The holiday season expresses the heart, soul, and history of the community. Barbara Kern describes the official opening of the Belleville Christmas season, saying, "The season begins the day after Thanksgiving with the annual Santa Claus parade. A large variety of bands, floats, and foot marchers, many dressed in costumes, parade down Main Street with Santa and Mrs. Claus bringing up the rear. Santa then is installed in the Santa Claus hut—made, decorated, and maintained by the Belleville Optimists—where he greets children who want to be sure he knows their desires for Christmas gifts." Children leave their holiday requests at the Santa House on the square before joining the annual Gingerbread Walk, where shopkeepers turn their store windows into an extended gallery to display gingerbread sculptures crafted by anyone old enough to make cookies. Bellevillians step back in time by taking a ride on an old-fashioned trolley tour of the city. The Historical Society also conducts an annual Holiday Candlelight house tour, with each home uniquely decorated by the home's owners.

On evenings between Thanksgiving and Christmas, a drive-through light show, "The Way of Lights," is presented by the National Shrine of Our Lady of the Snows. Begun in 1970, in part as a means of giving workers winter jobs, "The Way of Lights" extends for a mile and a half and now, in the twenty-first century, includes a laser show of the Christmas story.

A testament to Belleville's homage to tradition is its reputation for music. The Belleville Philharmonic Society and Orchestra, founded in 1866 by union veterans of German extraction just returned from fighting in the Civil War, is the nation's second oldest continuously performing orchestra and has provided holiday programs since 1867. The longevity of the Philharmonic was saluted by Illinois Representative Melvin Price, who entered a tribute to the Philharmonic's centennial celebration into the Congressional Record in 1967.

For the last twenty-five years, the Belleville Philharmonic Orchestra has joined forces with the Belleville School of Ballet for fully staged gala performances of Tchaikovsky's Nutcracker ballet. Guest dancers from leading American companies such as the American Ballet Theatre are brought in to dance the lead roles. The CD, *A Belleville Christmas*, was recorded by the Belleville Philharmonic Orchestra and Chorale in 2006. *Radiance of the Light*, a new Christmas cantata, was premiered by the Philharmonic Chorale and Orchestra in December 2007. The Philharmonic Chorale presents a concert each December called "Christmas Wonders," which traditionally concludes with a Christmas-carol "sing-along."

Many other fine ensembles are part of Belleville's musical scene. The Masterworks Chorale, founded by Dr. Dennis Sparger in 1978, and the Metro East Community Chorale, founded in 1992, include distinguished Christmas programs in their concert schedules. The Masterworks holiday offering, called "Christmas at the Cathedral," takes place in St. Peter's Cathedral in downtown Belleville. The area's churches have established deep-rooted traditions of their own that celebrate with holiday programs utilizing the talents of their congregations.

Musical theater is part of Belleville's holiday spirit as well and, as with other musical groups, is participated in by citizens of all backgrounds. For example, Dr. Charles DuMontier, a prominent radiologist, has followed the path of others before him who have made outstanding contributions to the arts. Dr. DuMontier has written a new Christmas musical, *Miracles*, to be premiered in December 2010, complete with orchestra, staging, and costuming. The common thread that unites the performing arts in Belleville is the spirit of community. Audiences are not surprised to find their doctor, teacher, librarian, dentist, or accountant giving their all on stage. At all levels, from leadership and creativity to vocal and instrumental section members, performers keep the pulse and infrastructure of the community strong and steady during the day and serve its artistic and spiritual life in the evening through their devotion and service to the arts. Julius Liese, the Belleville Philharmonic's second conductor, was also the founder of Liese Lumber, for decades "Belleville's premier lumber supplier."

Belleville reveres its history and heritage, and its citizens have mastered the art of throwing great parties and festivals to acknowledge and rejoice in the blessings of community. The Christmas season shows Belleville at its festive best.

Millikin's Gift: The Story of Vespers

TIMOTHY M. KOVALCIK

The fortunes of two Millikin Vespers traditions, one gone by and the other resoundingly successful, reflect the vicissitudes of Christmas traditions throughout Illinois—how one may disappear and how another has survived. Traditions such as these, described by history professor Dr. Timothy Kovalcik, are established throughout communities where town and gown unite in holiday celebrations.

In December 1959, 125 people came to Albert Taylor Theatre on the campus of Millikin University in Decatur. They were there as witnesses to "Vespers," a small but engaging Christmas concert. The evening's program included the university choir, the local children's choir from Westminster Presbyterian church, and several members of the art department. It was a humble but ambitious event. Its designers intended to bring the music alive with movement, decoration, and drama. As such, it was more than a simple choral concert; it was a visual treat that utilized more senses than just the aural capacity of the audience. Not one of these witnesses or any of the participants realized that this was the first of a new area-wide tradition. In fact, after five decades, seven thousand people a year now attend Vespers. Many fans claim that the Christmas season does not begin until Vespers weekend, during which Millikin hosts a minimum of three concerts. Directors spend their summer planning the event, and choirs practice for months in preparation. It has become part of the seasonal fabric in Decatur and is an important connection between "town and gown" in central Illinois.

The tradition of Vespers has continued for over fifty years. But another tradition lasting from 1921–32 was remarkably similar in purpose and intent. In 1921, Dean Arthur E. Wald proposed at a faculty meeting that the administration give the student body a Christmas gift in the form of a concert. This idea was enthusiastically received, a committee was formed, and plans were made for an elaborate staging of the Christmas story. Word spread quickly, and the campus turned out for the concert with friends and family. A new tradition had been born. A tableau inspired by Italian architecture and artwork became a centerpiece of the program, the scene created by talent from several departments, including art, music, and religion.

Millikin Vespers tableau, 1932

Millikin Vespers, 1992

Although Vespers was initially a success, as the Depression enveloped Decatur, the event began to wane. In 1932, the faculty announced that there would be no Vespers. An editorial in the student newspaper complained that the explanations from the administration for the tradition's demise were unsatisfactory. The editors concluded that the "potent factor" in the death of the tradition was "a lack of interest" on the part of the faculty committee. The students expressed their disappointment cynically: "Thus,

LIVING TRADITIONS ✦

Vespers, always beautiful in color and music, is denied us; a chapel, always dull and uneventful, is cheerfully granted us."

Eighteen years later, Richard Hoffland, a professor with new ideas and a new inspiration, created a new tradition that captured the intent of the original Vespers in its entirety. His goal was to provide Millikin and the community with a gift of music and art, a living concert that would bring Christmas alive. Before coming to Millikin University in 1959, Hoffland and his wife Kay were students of Paul Christiansen, a renowned choral director at Concordia College in Moorhead, Minnesota. At Concordia he created an annual Christmas concert that grew in reputation and complexity. The event incorporated not only college choirs but various elements of the campus and the surrounding community. Based on this experience, the Hofflands brought to Millikin a similar idea. While the Decatur community expected the traditional singing of Handel's *Messiah*, Professor Hoffland thought it especially important that students and the community be exposed to different sounds and types of music. In this regard the event was meant to be a celebration of the season, creating new experiences for the community by combining the traditional and contemporary.

With such a simple vision, the Hofflands were not constrained by the dictates of convention. They incorporated elements from various academic departments and included Westminster Presbyterian's children's choir, where Professor Hoffland was also director of music. Kay Hoffland remembers that there was "no guaranteed audience, so they both felt it essential to include a local choir," hoping to appeal to the community. Furthermore, there was no charge for admission. It was meant to be a simple gift that presented the best of the Millikin community and the sentiment of Christmas.

The teamwork of the Hofflands cannot be overstated. In 1932 one of the reasons cited by the administration for canceling Vespers was the retirement of faculty who had inspired the event. For over thirty years, the Hofflands personally insured that the event would not die. Their personalities were perfect for the job, and they helped maintain the tradition by choosing the music, designing the sets, and paying for expenses. They even hand-picked the dozens of Christmas trees that were used every year, and they developed local connections that helped promote the event in the Decatur area.

Vespers has been both a choral and visual event. The Hofflands experimented with floating Christmas trees, falling snow, and directors who "rose from the depths" as they used mechanical platforms to rise above the orchestra. In recent years, under the direction of Brad Holmes, Vespers was shaped by the use of a new Kirkland Fine Arts Center. Choirs not only sing. They move. They march. They appear, disappear, and reappear—all creating an effect that makes the spirit of the music come alive with movement.

Vespers is a medieval term signifying evening prayers. While the music affords a joyous occasion, the audience is introspective, appreciative, and dignified. Students in the choirs are trained to lift their heads proudly and keep their bodies motionless. They process and recess in perfect time, never missing a step while they simultaneously keep control of the pitch. This is what the audience is supposed to see: the spirit of Christmas perfectly matched with theme, presentation, and choral achievement.

To achieve such precision, participants, like atheletes, start in as soon as school convenes in the fall. When they return from Thanksgiving break, like their fellow students, they are faced with semester papers, recitals, and senior projects. In the midst of this frenzy, they spend every evening in Vespers. Combined choir pieces must come together, and students have to be trained in their movement. It is a grind. But, amazingly, this is what makes Vespers a memorable event for the performers. The distinguished fraternity of Vespers alumni increases with every annual performance, but initiation and the badge of honor are earned during rehearsal week.

While the Hofflands are responsible for establishing the tradition, Brad and Beth Holmes have continued to make the event special. Following the retirement of Dick Hoffland in 1990, they made an immediate impact by reevaluating the types of music used and the level of involvement from each choir. Under their direction the popularity of Vespers continues to grow. Now professional musicians and stage managers complement student and faculty participants. Multiple concerts are scheduled, and a small memorabilia market has emerged in the form of Vespers Christmas ornaments and programs. An additional choir director, Dr. Guy Forbes, has helped direct the program since 1994. All the choral directors have become producers, engineers, designers, and artists, embodying what Dick and Kay Hoffland envisioned as a combination of music, talent, and Christmas spirit.

To the Decatur community Vespers remains a simple and humble work of art, a gift to generations of central Illinoisans who consider it to be an enduring tradition.

Augustana Christmas Traditions

KAI SWANSON

Augustana College in Rock Island hosts a variety of Swedish Christmas celebrations, making it a popular destination for both town and gown during the holidays.

An institution collects a fair number of traditions over the course of 150 years, and Augustana College in Rock Island—founded in 1860—is no exception. Christmas is a time when special customs take center stage, which is probably a reflection of the college's Swedish Lutheran roots. But Augustana is also every inch an American institution, and that means new traditions are always being added.

One of the oldest Christmas traditions at Augustana is the Julsmörgåsbord, or Christmas feast. Long tables groan under the weight of smoked salmon, potato sausage, salads, pickled beets, and more types of herring than you may have thought existed. Bondost, or farmer cheese—pretty plain fare in Sweden—is celebrated as a delicacy and served with hardtack and Swedish rye. The meal ends with a cornucopia of cookies—what Swedish cuisine lacks in the realm of spicy is more than adequately made up for in sweets—and the traditional rice pudding with lingonberries.

"Smörgåsbord" means, literally, "butter-table," and reflects the Swedish practice of entire communities coming together to share food—a kind of Old World potluck, if you will. Once upon a time there would be just one of these feasts for the whole college, held prior to the Christmas recess, but today there are four each year, for employees, for area clergy, for special guests, and for the community at large.

A highlight of the employee smörgåsbord occurs after dessert, when all of the children of young faculty and staff adjourn to the college's Board Room. Each child takes a role in a very special telling of the Christmas story by Alvina Hanson, a retired teacher. With a doll standing in for the infant Jesus, children take the roles of Joseph, Mary, magi, shepherds, and the entire menagerie of manger animals, and everyone joins in punctuating Mrs. Hanson's story with such favorites as "O Little Town of Bethlehem," "Silent Night," "Hark, the Herald Angels Sing," and "Joy to the World."

Then, by strict tradition, the faculty pianist segues into "Jingle Bells" just in time for an appearance by the American version of Sweden's Jultomte, our jolly ol' Saint Nick, often portrayed by a faculty member chosen in part for not being a stranger to the aforementioned cookies. As if by magic, Santa knows the names of every child in attendance and even has a small pre-Christmas present for those who've been particularly good.

Though much more restrained, the clergy smörgåsbord also includes lots of singing. Vocal skill was expected of the pastors in the former Augustana Lutheran Synod, and it's been said it takes only three Augustana pastors to achieve eight-part harmony. It's a fitting start for the evening, which segues into another of the college's oldest traditions, George Frederick Handel's *Messiah*. First presented by Augustana's Handel Oratorio Society in 1881, the annual performance involves several hundred musicians, singers, and soloists and makes the Society one of the nation's oldest continuously operating musical ensembles.

The roots of *Messiah* at Augustana go back to April 4, 1879, when a professor and future president of Augustana College, Olof Olsson, heard *Messiah* performed at Exeter Hall in London. "I bought the cheapest ticket and mingled with the vast multitude gathered that evening," Olsson later wrote. "I will not attempt to describe the whole event, for I am not able. At times I was so carried away that I was hardly aware of myself. When the whole choir and orchestra came to the chorus, 'He shall be called Wonderful, Counsellor, God,' it penetrated to the marrow and bone and I feared I could not overcome the trembling."

The work made such a profound impression on him that upon his return to Rock Island, he set about trying to mount a production of Handel's masterpiece here. Finally in 1881 he succeeded, and the Handel Oratorio Society was born. In its first four decades, *Messiah* was performed only sporadically, alternating with other great works from the oratorio tradition. But since 1916—with only two exceptions—it's been performed at Augustana College every December.

Another vibrant link to the past takes students by the busload to the small town of Andover, Illinois, some twenty-five miles southeast of Rock Island. Andover is home to the first church established in North America by Lars Paul Esbjörn, Augustana's founding president, and for decades it has drawn students, faculty, staff, and community members from across the region for a tradition called "Joy of Christmas, Past and Present."

Beginning in the Augustana Lutheran church—an oversized structure for such a small town, reflecting its founders' firm belief that it would be the "mother church" for all Swedes in the New World—the worship service includes international students reading the Christmas story from the Gospel of Luke in their native languages. Over the years this has included French, Spanish, German, Arabic, Russian, Vietnamese,

Slovakian, Czech, Polish, Norwegian, Danish, Italian, Chinese, Hindi, Kiswahili, and (you guessed it) Swedish. The Augustana Chapel Choir then leads a candlelight procession past an old pioneer cemetery to the Jenny Lind Chapel, built by Esbjörn's flock in 1854 with contributions from the "Swedish Nightingale."

There, enveloped by candlelight and familiar carols played on a nineteenth-century pump organ, communion is celebrated. That holy feast is followed by a more secular one, as the students head back for mounds of cookies baked by the women of Augustana Lutheran church.

No December in a Swedish-American community would be complete without Sankta Lucia. Adopted by Swedes in the 1800s and built loosely around the tale of a fourth-century Sicilian girl who was martyred for her faith, the Swedish Luciafest includes a young woman with a crown of pine branches and candles, attended by white-clad girls and wand-toting *stjerngossar,* or "star boys," all of whom make their appearance at the various julsmörgåsbords. As one of the few U.S. colleges to offer a major in Swedish language and literature, Augustana's celebration centers on Lucia and her retinue singing traditional Swedish Christmas songs (while quietly being graded on their pronunciation).

Although new by Augustana standards, the college is also home to one of the oldest collegiate celebrations of Kwanzaa you'll find, having been observed at Augustana for more than thirty years. Since Kwanzaa, like Christmas, actually falls during the recess when students are home with their families, this observance likewise falls a little early, but allows the campus "family" to come together in celebration.

A somewhat newer tradition, though one that's rapidly becoming the most popular, is an annual Service of Lessons and Carols in the college's Ascension Chapel, featuring the Augustana Chamber Singers under its director, Dr. Jon Hurty, who also directs the Handel Oratorio Society and the Augustana Choir, and thereby continues a tradition in choral music almost as old as the college itself.

Never forgetting that Augustana is, after all, a learning institution, another of the venerable customs at the college delves into the realm of science. The annual "Season of Light" program at Augustana's John Deere Planetarium has been a fixture since the facility opened in 1968 with a dedicatory lecture by none other than Neil Armstrong. The program, which draws hundreds of people each December, explores the ways in which ancient cultures—including Hebrew, Celtic, and Roman, among others—attempted to bring light to the dark days of midwinter, and considers the science behind the Bible's Star of Bethlehem.

Youngsters Learn Polish Christmas Custom

ROCKFORD OBSERVER

*Christmas traditions, such as the eating of the "oplatek," described in
this 1989 article, are handed down from generation to generation and
are rigorously adhered to.*

"No, no, Steve. Don't eat your wafer. Break a little off
Andy's and eat it. Now Andy, you break a little off of
Steve's."

Janina Korab, grandmother of the two young Korab
boys, is showing her grandsons an old Polish custom.

Steve reaches for his brother's wafer, called "oplatek" in Polish. It looks and tastes
like a communion host, but is larger and has an oblong shape. He breaks off a piece
and eats it.

Father John Mikula, pastor at St. Stanislaus Kostka Parish in Rockford, is watching as grandma instructs her grandchildren. He explains that the custom of exchanging the Christmas wafer is one of both greeting and forgiveness.

The old Polish custom gives people an opportunity to extend best wishes for the
holiday season and clear the slate as the new year approaches.

"As you offer the wafer you ask for forgiveness of past difficulties," said Father
Mikula.

The wafer is exchanged on Christmas Eve. Mrs. Korab describes the scene. There
is a big dinner—twelve courses, all meatless.

A little hay is put under the tablecloth to remind everyone that Jesus was born in
a stable. There is an extra place for an unexpected guest. Before sitting down to eat,
everyone says a prayer together.

Then each person takes a piece of oplatek. The oldest person in the room begins
the ritual by exchanging oplatek with the person next to him or her. Then everyone
else does the same, exchanging oplatek and seasonal greetings of peace.

Crumbs are shared with the family pet—or on farms, with animals in the barn.

As the priest speaks, the two youngsters practice sharing oplatek under grandma's
watchful eye. If practice makes perfect, they'll have it right when the Korab clan gath-
ers Christmas Eve.

Tradition and Maud Martha

GWENDOLYN BROOKS

Maud Martha *is Gwendolyn Brooks's coming-of-age story of an African American woman in 1940s Chicago whose memory of Christmas contains universal themes.*

W
hat she had wanted was a solid. She had wanted shimmering form; warm, but hard as stone and as difficult to break. She had wanted to found—tradition. She had wanted to shape, for their use, for hers, for his, for little Paulette's, a set of falterless customs. She had wanted stone: here she was, being wife to him, salving him, in every way considering replenishing him—in short, here she was celebrating Christmas night by passing pretzels and beer.

He had done his part, was his claim. He had, had he not? lugged in a Christmas tree. So he had waited till early Christmas morning, when a tree was cheap; so he could not get the lights to burn; so the tinsel was insufficient and the gold balls few. He had promised a tree and he had gotten a tree, and that should be enough for everybody. Furthermore, Paulette had her blocks, her picture book, her doll buggy and her doll. So the doll's left elbow was chipped: more than that would be chipped before Paulette was through! And if the doll buggy was not like the Gold Coast buggies, that was too bad; that was too, too bad for Maud Martha, for Paulette. Here he was whipping himself to death daily, that Maud Martha's stomach and Paulette's stomach might receive bread and milk and navy beans with tomato catsup, and he was taken to task because he had not furnished, in addition, a velvet-lined buggy with white-walled wheels! Oh yes, that *was* what Maud Martha wanted, for her precious princess daughter, and no use denying. But she could just get out and work, that was all. She could just get out and grab herself a job and buy some of these beans and buggies. And in the meantime, she could just help entertain his friends. She was his wife, and he was the head of the family, and on Christmas night the least he could do, by God, and *would* do, by God, was stand his friends a good mug of beer. And to heck with, in fact, to hell with, her fruitcakes and coffees. Put Paulette to bed.

At Home, the buying of the Christmas tree was a ritual. Always it had come into the Brown household four days before Christmas, tall, but not too tall, and not too wide. Tinsel, bulbs, little Santa Clauses and snowmen, and the pretty gold and silver colored balls did not have to be renewed oftener than once in five years, because after Christmas, they were always put securely away on a special shelf in the basement, where they rested for a year. Black walnut candy, in little flat white sheets, crunchy, accompanied the tree, but it was never eaten until Christmas eve. Then, late at night, a family decorating party was held, Maud Martha, Helen and Harry giggling and teasing and occasionally handing up a ball or Santa Claus, while their father smiled benignly over all and strung and fitted and tinseled, and their mother brought in the black walnut candy and steaming cups of cocoa with whipped cream, and plain shortbread. And everything peaceful, sweet!

Un Poquito de Tu Amor

SANDRA CISNEROS

A distinguished Latina Illinois writer fathoms her relationship with her father and her country within the context of the world in which she lives.

When my father died last year, a week before Valentine's Day, a piece of my heart died with him. My father, that supreme sentimental fool, loved my brothers and me to excess in a kind of over-the-top, rococo fever, all arabesques and sugar spirals, as sappy and charming as the romantic Mexican boleros he loved to sing. *Just a little bit of your love at least, / just a little bit of your love, just that.* . . . Music from my time, Father would say proudly, and I could almost smell the gardenias and Tres Flores hair oil.

Before my father died, it was simple cordiality that prompted me to say, "I'm sorry," when comforting the bereaved. But with his death I am initiated into the family of humanity, I am connected to all deaths and to their survivors: "*Lo siento,*" which translates as both "I am sorry" and "I feel it" all at once.

Lo siento. Since his death, I feel life more intensely.

My father, born under the eagle and serpent of the Mexican flag, died beneath a blanket of stars and stripes, a U.S. World War II veteran. Like most immigrants, he was overly patriotic, exceptionally hardworking, and, above all, a great believer in family. Yet often I'm aware my father's life doesn't count, he's not "history," not what the "American" politicians mean when they talk about "American."

I thought of my father especially this holiday season. The day before Christmas 1997, forty-five unarmed Mayas were slain while they prayed in a chapel in Acteal, Chiapas—twenty-one of them women, fourteen children. The Mexican president was shocked and promised to hold all those responsible accountable. The Mexican people aren't fools. Everybody knows who's responsible, but it's too much to wish for the Mexican president to fire himself.

I know the deaths in Chiapas are linked to me here in the United States. I know the massacre is connected to removing native people from their land, because although the people are poor the land is very rich and the government knows this. And the Mexican debt is connected to my high standard of living, and the military presence is necessary to calm U.S. investors, and the music goes round and round and it comes out here.

I have been thinking and thinking about all this from my home in San Antonio, Texas, as fidgety as a person with *comezón*, an itching, a hankering, an itch I can't quite scratch. What is my responsibility as a writer in light of these events? As a woman, as a mestiza? As a U.S. citizen who lives on several borders? What do I do as the daughter of a Mexican man? Father, tell me. *Ayúdame*, help me, why don't you. *Lo siento.* I have been searching for answers. On Christmas, I am reverberating like a bell.

In my father's house, because my father was my father—*Hello, my friend!*—our Christmas dinners were a global feast, a lesson in history, diplomacy, and the capacity of the stomach to put aside racial grievances. Our holidays were a unique hybrid of cultures that perhaps could only happen in a city like Chicago, a bounty contributed by family and intermarriage, multiethnic neighborhoods, and the diversity of my father's upholstery-shop employees.

To this day, a typical Christmas meal at our home consists first and foremost of tamales, that Indian delicacy that binds us to the preconquest. Twenty-five dozen for our family is typical, the popular red tamales, the fiery green tamales, and the sweet, pink tamales filled with jam and raisins for the kids. Sometimes they're my mother's home-made batch—*This is the last year I'm going to make them!*—but more often they're ordered in advance from someone willing to go through all the trouble, most recently from the excellent tamale lady in front of Carnicería Jiménez on North Avenue, who operates from a shopping cart.

Father's annual contribution was his famous *bacalao*, a codfish stew of Spanish origin, which he made standing in one spot like a TV chef—*Go get me a bowl, bring me an apron, somebody give me the tomatoes, wash them first, hand me that knife and chopping board, where are the olives?*

Every year we are so spoiled we expect—and receive—a Christmas tray of home-made pierogis and Polish sausage, sometimes courtesy of my sister-in-law's family, the Targonskis, and sometimes from my father's Polish upholsterers, who can hardly speak a word of English. We also serve Jamaican meat pies, a legacy from Darryl, who was once father's furniture refinisher, but has long since left. And finally, our Christmas dinner includes the Italian magnificence from Ferrara Bakery in our old neighborhood on West Taylor Street. Imagine if a cake looked like the Vatican. We've been eating Ferrara's pastries since I was in the third grade.

But this is no formal Norman Rockwell sit-down dinner. We eat when we're inspired by hunger or by *antojo*, literally "before the eye." All day pots are on the stove steaming and the microwave is beeping. It's common to begin a dessert plate of cannolis while someone next to you is finishing breakfast, a pork tamale sandwiched inside a piece of French bread, a mestizo invention thanks to the French intervention.

History is present at our table. The doomed Emperor Maximiliano's French bread as well as the Aztec corn tamales of the Americas, our Andalusian recipe for codfish, our moves in and out of the neighborhoods where we were the brown corridor between Chicago communities at war with one another. And finally a history of intermarriage, of employees who loved my father enough to share a plate of their home-made delicacies with our family even if our countries couldn't share anything else.

Forty-five are dead in Acteal. My father is gone. I read the newspapers and the losses ring in my heart. More than half the Mexican-American kids in this country are dropping out of high school—more than half—and our politicians' priority is bigger prisons. I live in a state where there are more people sentenced to death than anywhere else in the world. Alamo Heights, the affluent, white neighborhood of my city, values Spanish as a second language beginning in the first grade, yet elsewhere lawmakers work to demolish bilingual education for Spanish-dominant children. Two hours away from my home, the U.S. military is setting up camp in the name of bandits and drug lords. But I'm not stupid; I know who they mean to keep away. *Lo siento.* I feel it.

I'm thinking this while I attend a Latino leadership conference between the holidays. I don't know what I expect from this gathering of Latino leaders, exactly, but I know I don't want to leave without a statement about what's happened in Acteal. Surely at least the Latino community recognizes the forty-five are our family.

"It is like a family," one Arizona politico explains. "But understand, to you it may be a father who's died, but to me it's a distant cousin."

Is it too much to ask our leaders to lead?

"You're too impatient," one Latina tells me, and I'm so stunned I can't respond. A wild karaoke begins, and a Chicano filmmaker begins to preach—There's a season to play and a season to rage. He talks and talks till I have to blink back the tears. After what seems like an eternity, he finally finishes by saying, "You know what you have to do, don't you?"

And then it hits me, I do know what I have to do.

I will tell a story.

When we were in college my mother realized investing in real estate was the answer to our economic woes. Her plans were modest: to buy a cheap fixer-upper in the barrio that would bring us income. After months of searching, Mother finally found something we could afford, a scruffy building on the avenue with a store that could serve as Father's upholstery shop and two apartments above that would pay the mortgage. At last my mother was a respectable landlady.

Almost immediately a family on the third floor began paying their rent late. It wasn't an expensive apartment, something like a hundred dollars, but every first of the month, they were five or ten dollars short and would deliver the rent with a promise to pay the balance the next payday, which they did. Every month it was the same . . . the rent minus a few dollars promised for next Friday.

Mother hated to be taken advantage of. *Do they think we're rich or something, don't we have bills too?* She sent Father, who was on good terms with everybody. *You go and talk to that family, I've had it!*

And so Father went, and a little later quietly returned.

"I fixed it," Father announced.

"Already? How? What did you do?"

"I lowered the rent."

Mother was ready to throw a fit. Until Father said, "Remember when ten dollars meant a lot to us?"

Mother was silent, as if by some *milagro* she remembered. Who would've thought Father was capable of such genius? He was not by nature a clever man. But he inspires me now to be creative in ways I never realized.

I don't wish to make my Father seem more than what he was. He wasn't Gandhi; he lived a life terrified of those different from himself. He never read a newspaper and was naive enough to believe history as told by *la televisión*. And, as my mother keeps reminding me, he wasn't a perfect husband either. But he was very kind and at some things extraordinary. He was a wonderful father.

Maybe I've looked to the wrong leaders for leadership. Maybe what's needed this new year are a few outrageous ideas. Something absurd and genius like those of my father, whose kindness and generosity teach me to enlarge my heart.

Maybe it's time to lower the rent.

Just a little bit of your love at least, / just a little bit of your love, just that . . . ever since the year began that song runs through my head. My father just won't let up. *Lo siento.* I feel it.

Papá, Buddha, Allah, Jesus Christ, Yahweh, La Virgen de Guadalupe, the Universe, the God in us, help us. *Danos un poquito de tu amor siquiera, danos un poquito de tu amor nomás* . . . just a little bit of your love at least, just a little bit of your love, just that . . .

Songs and Symbols

Christmas Trees

JOHN W. ALLEN

Tree decorations, whether gaudy, religious, or artful, are the reason to seek out from the Christmas stand in town or the tree farmer's field the best-shaped tree possible. Few trees today grow in natural locations—there are laws against cutting them—and fewer still are decorations that are homespun. Both trees and ornaments today are, as one would say a century ago, "boughten." And supposedly, they come fireproofed.

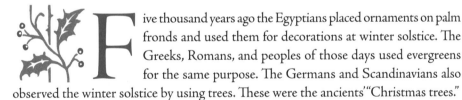 ive thousand years ago the Egyptians placed ornaments on palm fronds and used them for decorations at winter solstice. The Greeks, Romans, and peoples of those days used evergreens for the same purpose. The Germans and Scandinavians also observed the winter solstice by using trees. These were the ancients' "Christmas trees."

In the 1500s Martin Luther decorated and lighted a small evergreen in his home and thus made it a part of the world's Christmas legend.

The first decorated tree recorded for Illinois was one that the daughters of Gustave Koerner decorated at Belleville in 1833. They took "the top of a young sassafras which still had some leaves on it . . . dressed it with ribbon and bits of colored paper and the like" and "hung it with little red apples and nuts and all sorts of confections" made by

Facing page:
Christmas
1915, Peoria
County

Christmas 1900, Union County

"Aunt Caroline.""They put waxed candles on the branches," Koerner says. "Perhaps this is the first Christmas [tree] that was lighted on the banks of the Mississippi."

Much later, about 1900, trees became country-wide in use. Today eight out of ten houses in America have them.

Trees and trimmings can be bought now at countless places. When the custom began, both were homemade. This brief story of the first one in a rural district school will tell something of many others.

A farmer gave a small cedar tree, and the teacher sent larger boys to cut and bring it to the school a day or two prior to its use. To the boys, going half a mile for the tree, then carrying and dragging it back, was not a task but a privilege.

Its decoration on the day before its use was a grand occasion. White cloth and cotton batting were arranged under the tree to represent snow. A pupil-made cardboard fireplace, with mantle and knitted wool socks, was placed near the tree.

The tree was lighted by candles tied to its branches with string or attached with clothespins. Brilliantly colored crepe paper was cut into strips for drapes. Many yards of strung popcorn crisscrossed the tree. A bag of red cranberries made a long string that hung from the branches. Red haws made other strings, and clusters of the small red fruit of the buckberry with rusty rose pips were tied in place. Spiny fruits of the sweet gum tree were covered with tin foil saved from plug chewing tobacco. Surplus foil was cut into narrow strips to drape on branches or into small bits to make artificial snow. Glistening baubles hung from the branches, and a shiny foil-covered star was fastened at the very top of the tree. Bits of cotton looked like patches of snow. Expressed mildly, it made a first-class fireball.

Gifts were plainly wrapped, and names were written on them. They were tied on the tree, not stacked beneath.

A special program was arranged. It consisted of readings, recitations, songs, and a short dialogue. Among the numbers offered were: "Silent Night," "O Little Town of Bethlehem," "Jolly Saint Nicholas," "While Shepherds Watched Their Flocks at Night," "'Twas the Night before Christmas," "It Came upon a Midnight Clear," and that ever-popular poem where each stanza ended with "'Ceptin' jes' 'fore Christmas I'm as good as I can be." Others are forgotten.

Parents came to enjoy the program. Santa Claus with jingling bells and a tied-on cotton beard came dressed in the regular oversized, pillow-stuffed, red cotton suit to take the gifts from the tree and call names in a thinly disguised voice. He frightened the very young, thrilled the next age group, puzzled some beyond that, and dispelled the Santa myth with those sure of his identity.

University of Illinois Madrigal Singers

The teacher also passed out the annual treat of oranges or apples and candy. This brought all pupils enrolled, even those who had dropped out.

The old-time, homemade, country Christmas tree has passed, but has left pleasant memories. It also left many a story of tragedy when trees caught fire and children were burned to death. Old files of the Christmas issues of newspapers carry many such stories.

Christmas still belongs to children, but memories of it belong to oldsters.

Songs of Good Cheer

MARY SCHMICH AND ERIC ZORN

Traditions are what people deem worth repeating from year to year, and they usually stem from an idea fostered by one or two people. Few contemporary Christmas traditions in Illinois have been as satisfyingly successful as the Songs of Good Cheer, an event put on by Chicago's Old Town School of Folk Music. With good cheer Mary Schmich planted the seed, and in good humor Eric Zorn helped it grow.

Hark! Why Isn't Anyone Singing Christmas Carols?

MARY SCHMICH, DECEMBER 23, 1998

Somewhere out there, someone must be caroling.

Somewhere in this Christmas season, ordinary people are gathered in living rooms or on sidewalks, their voices soaring through "Joy to the World," dipping low for "Silent Night," then joining in tight harmony for "O Come All Ye Faithful."

But where?

Sure, the tunes are out there. On the radio, in the malls, on the stereo as background noise at parties. But who's singing them? I mean really singing? How many ordinary folks are breaking into full-throttled renditions of "O Holy Night," straining unashamedly for that impossible high?

Christians of various stripes still sing carols in church, but that's not the kind of free-for-all caroling I mean. I mean singing as a rite not so much of worship as of friendship, caroling that is less about denominational conviction than community.

When I was in grade school, then in college, and at a Christmas party for a while after that, crowds would gather around a piano and belt out the great songs of Christmas. For some of the singers, the songs were an expression of religious ecstasy. But for just as many, the pleasure lay in the taut lyrics and lyrical melodies. These were songs that felt good on the tongue and in the heart, independent of their religious roots. You could belt out "Angels We Have Heard on High" without believing in angels, though the great sweeping melody of that song could make even a doubter a believer, at least until the song's last note.

Certain lines of so many of these songs could put a lump in almost any throat. "A thrill of hope / the weary world rejoices / for yonder breaks a new and glorious morn." Today, as I hear that line from "O Holy Night," I imagine a world in which the United States and Iraq lay down their arms, in which Palestine and Israel become true friends, in which those guys in Congress withdraw their fangs. In other years, I've heard it other ways. In any year, it's powerful.

The songs of Christmas, of course, include those without religious reference beyond the reference to Christmas itself. "Silver Bells," "White Christmas," and the heart-rending "Jingle Bell Rock" all belong in the repertoire. But even the best of the secular Christmas songs can't compete with the artistry of the great religious carols. For whatever reason, the songs inspired by faith are simply better songs.

Great carols, like great songs of any kind, have the power to move whoever hears or sings them. Their power transcends literal analysis. Singing them with others gives them even greater force.

But outside churches and the occasional party, collective Christmas caroling has fallen casualty to the peculiarities and sensitivities of our age. Many schools, fearful of offending non-Christians, have axed carols from the activities. In urban neighborhoods where people don't know their neighbors, assembling a caroling crew is harder than ever. Who knows which cranky neighbor will call the cops complaining about a disturbance of the peace?

Add to that the omnipresence of recorded music. By saturating our lives with music made by others, I'm convinced, recorded music has deterred many of us from making our own.

"Do you sing Christmas carols?" I asked a friend the other day.

"If you mean like under my breath with the radio when I'm at home?" she said. "Yeah. Otherwise? No. My family used to sing them together when I was a kid. But not anymore."

I considered having a Christmas carol party this year. But what if people, increasingly unaccustomed to singing in public, were too embarrassed to sing? Besides, so many of them are Jewish.

Shortly after I'd abandoned the idea, a friend mentioned she wanted to go Christmas caroling. She is Jewish. When I expressed surprise, she explained she'd grown up singing carols. They remind her of her childhood. She thinks of them less as Christmas songs or Christian songs than as "winter carols."

Far more people than we know, I suspect, yearn to sing at Christmastime. Surely there's a way to restore more singing for the season. Singing together is a kind of social glue. We need the bond of the winter carols in this weary world.

Jingle Belle Gets a Challenge from Old Holy Knight

ERIC ZORN, OCTOBER 17, 1999

I'm calling your bluff.

In late December last year, you wrote one of those evocative, things-jes'-ain't-the-way-they-used-to-be columns—and nobody does them better—about Christmas carols. "Outside churches and the occasional party, collective Christmas caroling has fallen casualty to the peculiarities and sensitivities of our age," you wrote. Then later, "Surely there's a way to restore more singing to the season. Singing together is a kind of social glue. We need the bond of the winter carols in this weary world."

Well, Mary, no sooner had I finished dabbing my eyes than I decided to suit up my actions to your words. And now the plans are taking shape.

On your behalf, I have reserved the spectacular new Old Town School of Folk Music auditorium for the night of December 17. I have arranged for a piano on stage for you to play so we can approximate your memories of the days when "crowds would gather around a piano and belt out the great songs of Christmas."

I have started assembling a booklet of lyrics for the evening—you seem fond of "O Holy Night," but can you sing it without shattering the windows?—and enlisted the aid, both on- and offstage, of experienced performers and song leaders such as Valerie Mindel, Mike Miller, and Barbara Silverman to make sure things go well.

I'll join you on stage with my assortment of hillbilly instruments and emotive vocal stylings ("Anyone can sing in tune," to paraphrase Oscar Wilde, "but I sing with wonderful expression"), and for a couple of hours we'll lead anyone else who shows up in singing "full-throttled renditions," as you longed for, of the greatest seasonal carols. The Tribune Holiday Fund, for which "Do-It-Yourself-Schmich" will be a benefit, is still working out all the little details. Time. Donation/ticket price. Which of us gets the bigger dressing room.

So, will you be there? Or was all that about "songs that [feel] good on the tongue and the heart" just so much verbiage to fill up this space?

And, hey, thanks for inviting me over to the Sunday paper to begin one of our periodic weeks of correspondence. Aren't you going to introduce me to your friends?

Mr. Ho Ho Ho

GRINCH SCHMICH, OCTOBER 17, 1999

You know, Eric, the only thing I hate more than a whiner is a doer. I was just whining when I wrote that column about Christmas carols. Complaining is a very important columnist function—the essential one, in fact—and I heartily agree with a revered former *New York Times* editor who once grumbled to me, "Columnists! All talk, no action!"

So, while I truly, deeply miss the kind of communal Christmastime singing that exists in my romantic memories, I never, ever intended to do anything about it, particularly not something that would expose my mediocre musicianship on a stage in the Old Town School of Folk Music.

Now you've roped me into a public spectacle, just as you roped me into these occasional dialogue columns. (For Sunday readers who don't know, you and I alternate in this space Mondays through Fridays, except a couple of times a year when we cohabit for a week and whine in chorus.)

But it's good for me, a woman of whines and dreams, to be nudged by you, a man of action. So, I'll sign on to your scheme. I know there are lots of readers out there yearning to sing free. Many of them wrote me lyrical, inspiring letters after my lament for Christmas carols.

We should make it clear, by the way, that our little sing-along is for people of all faiths. It will be a celebration of the season for anyone who likes good tunes and good company. We should also make it clear that this is not an event that requires a good voice. If it were, I wouldn't be there.

It may seem early to announce an event for December 17, but we want people to know about this one before their December calendars are as gridlocked as O'Hare in a snowstorm.

So, I'm warming up my fingers and sorting through my tattered songbooks. My neighbors will probably call the cops or a psychiatrist soon, since I've taken to pounding out "Jingle Bell Rock" at odd hours in the middle of October.

Cheer Report

ERIC ZORN, DECEMBER 11, 2006

I move today for a temporary revision of the lyrics to "The Christmas Song"—in particular, the passage that extends best holiday wishes "to kids from one to ninety-two." Let's make it "kids from one to 102."

That way it will continue to fit the rhyme scheme while also including in the blanket greeting the great author, activist, and raconteur Studs Terkel, ninety-four, who made a surprise appearance Saturday night at the Songs of Good Cheer sing-along, taking the stage during the opening number, "Joy to the World."

It marked an exciting convergence of venerable Chicago institutions—Terkel, a living legend by any measure, and the Old Town School, which was founded forty-nine years ago by good friends of Terkel's. Terkel is one of the few surviving links to the humble origins of what's now a grand facility with an international reputation for presenting, preserving, and teaching roots music of all sorts.

Studs gave a short speech about the vision of his pal and performing companion Win Stracke, a cofounder of the school in 1957, then left us to fill the spectacular space with song and bit of silliness.

For the last eight years at about this time, Mary Schmich and I have hosted the "Songs . . ." programs at the school. She plays the piano. I play a couple of stringed instruments (only the guitar this year), and a cast of professional musicians joins us on stage to complete the sound and keep us in tune.

About 450 people jam the auditorium with songbooks in hand, and we fill the space with holiday-themed music.

Studs Terkel,
Songs of Good
Cheer, 2006, by
Steve Kagan

Hessel Park
Reformed
Church,
Champaign

Christmas Music in an Illinois Public School

THEODORE KLINKA

Songs and symbols of Christmas, particularly in Illinois institutions that serve all the public, have been altered over the years in the spirit of inclusivity. But, as Dr. Theodore Klinka, the former chair of music at New Trier High School, writes, the energy and talent of the young people who perform for large and appreciative audiences have not waned.

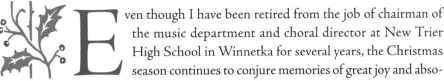

Even though I have been retired from the job of chairman of the music department and choral director at New Trier High School in Winnetka for several years, the Christmas season continues to conjure memories of great joy and absolute exhaustion. As with most of my colleagues who began their careers in the public schools in the mid-1950s, I spent part of the first semester of each school year preparing for the climactic December musical event that celebrated the birth of Christ. A director in a small community like LaPorte, Indiana, where I began teaching, might be expected to prepare three different Christmas choral programs for the school, church, and community. The audiences and voices differed a bit. The director remained the same. When I came to New Trier, I directed the Christmas Festival at the high school and at a church that presented an elaborate Christmas pageant. The requisite rehearsals led up to the concerts on the second Sunday in December. On that day, the pageant was enacted at 9:00 and 11:00 A.M. and 2:00 and 4:00 P.M. Less than three hours after the final pageant, the New Trier Festival began promptly at 8:00 P.M. I was always thankful that Christmas came but once a year.

Over the forty years I taught in the public schools, the season's pleasures and challenges remained, but school Christmas music celebrations began to change. Not only in the Midwest, but also throughout the nation, there was a perceptible evolution from music solely dedicated to celebrating Christ's birth to more secular programs that recognized a diverse population in the schools. School music directors were at the center of what often were controversial decisions. The Illinois Chapter of the American Choral Directors' Association, a group of professionals which I led as president, helped directors understand their role in managing the growing sensitivity to the separation of church and state. Tax-supported music departments in public schools had to consider their options. Some began to perform totally seasonal secular music or to perform music celebrating diverse ethnicities and religions. In some cases, schools eliminated December music concerts entirely.

New Trier High School typifies the evolution that has taken place. Immigrants from Trier, Germany, settled the area in the mid-1850s, and they were a dominant population when the school's orchestra was formed in 1901 and a glee club was added in 1908. The orchestra and choir presented its first Christmas concert in 1917, and in 1922 an annual Christmas concert was shared with the choir of Christ church in Winnetka. The repertoire of those early concerts was religious Christmas music, including numerous Christmas carols sung by the choirs and audience. The last shared carol of the evening was "Silent Night," a custom that continued into the early 1950s. A number of the Christmas concerts in the 1920s and 1930s also included performances of sacred Christmas cantatas relating the biblical story of Christmas and the reading of the Christmas lesson from the scriptures. As late as the 1950s, art department students participated in the Christmas Festival by creating a backdrop of artificial windows made to resemble stained-glass windows found in Christian churches and cathedrals. Some seven hundred choral members and two hundred members of the orchestra and band performed for an audience in the hall that normally served as the gymnasium. These nine hundred kids represented 20 percent of the student body of approximately 4,500.

A significant shift for New Trier Christmas programs began in the early 1960s, when the district built an additional school to accommodate increasing enrollment. This new building no doubt accelerated at New Trier a change that would become pervasive in Illinois public-school December concerts in the next few years. The student body of the new school included many Jewish students. Some Jewish parents and many Christian parents who understood that Jewish students and others who were not Christian were being asked to participate in a sectarian festival began a dialogue that led to a reevaluation of the whole concept of a "Christmas Festival." The result was not only a name change to a "Winter Music Festival" but also an increased focus on a balanced repertoire, including more secular seasonal music and the addition of significant Hebrew literature.

My students were never as concerned as their parents about our musical choices. One Jewish student even suggested that we could just perform the same music at both the early and late concerts, but just change all the titles. For example: "Away in a Manger" would become "Away with the Manger"; "Ave Maria" would become "Oy Vay Maria." Her classmates applauded.

*New Trier
Chorus and
Orchestra, 1953*

Like public schools across Illinois, New Trier continues to be sensitive to how it chooses religious music literature, not only at Christmas but throughout the year. The school follows comprehensive guidelines for the performance of religious music in public schools, adapted from the Music Educators' National Conference's recommendations. But as with all those schools that have adapted their musical performances to meet the changing times over the past century, the quality of the music, the celebration of the season, and the enjoyment of the performance by audiences, students, and, yes, even the exhausted directors continue unabated. The challenge of today's public school concerts, both musically and culturally, is something I could not have anticipated when I began as a wide-eyed young music educator who began thinking of a career in music, even when I was a teenage participant in the choir of a Milwaukee, Wisconsin, Missouri Synod Lutheran church.

Belinda Grey and the Christmas Carol

LADONNA HARRELL MARTIN

Folk-song traditions have been kept alive in southern Illinois by descendants of the first settlers, influencing the way they sing carols.

 It all began when I was about seventeen and a student at Southern Illinois University. Her name was Belinda Grey. She was old, tired, and shrunken, but she could sing.

The most beautiful, the most poignant Christmas song I've ever heard came from the heart and soul of that old, old woman.

She was seated in a willow rocking chair on the front porch of a log cabin, deep in the middle of what is now Shawnee National Forest.

That was in the forties. I was a student assistant to David McIntosh at SIU. Dr. McIntosh was a dedicated collector of southern Illinois folk music. He strolled the hills and back roads on weekends, trying to collect the jewels before they disappeared.

Somewhere south of Carbondale we turned left and from then on I was lost in the hills, awestruck with their beauty. I believe our destination was somwhere in Pope County.

Belinda sang for us all afternoon. She sang "Mary, Don't You Weep," "Adam in the Garden," "Poor Wayfaring Stranger," "O, Lovely Appearing of Death," "Go Tell It on the Mountain."

She needed no help with accompaniment. She just rocked the rhythm, patted or pounded the arm of her willow rocker.

But it was the last song she sang that was so acute to the spirit, so keenly piercing and, for a Christmas carol, so bitter: "Mary Was a Lady."

Before she began to sing it, she turned her rocker away from us, set herself straight staring out over the yard, the dirt road, the cedars, and up into the high ridge. Her face seemed impassive, her body quiet during this song:

> Mary was a lady, fine and fair,
> A-ver pleasant-lookin' and coal black hair.
> Mary, now, she gained old Joseph's mind,
> When he saw that woman an' she looked so fine.

But de Lawd had done blessed her for a little holy chile,
And Joseph didn't know if he could walk that mile.
But the angel came and put it right good in his mind,
And Mary went to Joseph in a fancy style.

CHORUS
But that old cold cave, it wuz so lonely,
And them old birth pangs, they wuz so bad.
It wuz the worstest bedding poor Mary ever had.
Seemed like death was a creepin' in that stall,
And a blood-red cross wuz a-hammered in the wall,
And a blood-red cross wuz a-hammered in the wall.

At the last chorus Belinda seemed to become frozen, completely unaffected by the suffering and pain in the impassioned words. The chorus began with a sudden long, high wail:

Oooooo, Joseph . . . hand me that baby.
Oooooo, Joseph . . . hand me that little baby,
Death creepin' through the door.
Oooooo, Joseph . . . lie down beside me,
Death hangin' on the wall,
Death hangin' on the wall.
Ain't nobody gonna care at all.

I guess the time and place were right, late in the afternoon, twilight approaching, dark-green cedars casting shadows across the road and the darkness of the heavy oaks and thickets up on the ridge. Dr. Mac sat in a chair beside Belinda. I was cross-legged on the porch floor, with two old red dogs lying near the porch steps.

Always before in his interviews, Dr. McIntosh had rushed right in after a song. Where did you learn it? When? Who? Why? All necessities for dedicated collectors. But this time Dr. Mac said nothing. He was a kind, serious man and very quiet when at ease. But he had learned how to interview these folk singers and in the past had always come up to his task.

But after this song, Belinda rocked and Dr. Mac sat.

The high lonesome wail of the "Oooooo, Joseph" that had pierced the twilight gloom still lingered like an echo. But the low, spoken, "Aint' nobody gonna care at all,"

*Christmas tree, by
May Theilgaard Watts*

were the first words I'd ever heard that reached me about the reality of man's inability to love God.

Belinda said her mother brought the song up from one of the Carolinas (she didn't know which), and she said she thought she'd lost some lines and maybe a verse or two.

When we rose to leave, Belinda said, "God bless ye . . . ain't no song worth cryin' over."

That was the day I began to fall in love with southernmost southern Illinois.

I came from a land of long, long rows of corn and soybeans, planted in long flat eighty-acre fields. But these hills, these people, offered something the cornfields lacked.

SONGS AND SYMBOLS ✦

A String of Lights for Christmas

ROBERT J. HASTINGS

*In this recollection, the songs and symbols of Christmas brought surcease
from the effects of the Great Depression in Marion in Williamson County.*

Christmas at 1404 North State began when Mom reached for the cardboard box marked "Xmas decorations" on the top shelf of the pantry. First to go up were the ropes of paper garlands, green and red, which she stretched across the living and dining rooms. Where the strands crossed in the center of each room, she suspended a big, red paper bell which folded out like an old-fashioned Valentine heart. From the ropes we hung silvery icicles; in the windows we put red paper wreathes.

Tree ornaments, carefully packed away from previous years, were unwrapped. These included some frayed icicles, brittle with age, which seemed to get shorter each year. If the little metal loop on an ornament was broken, cotton string or hairpins held it to the tree.

White divinity candy and fresh fruit salad were two Christmas musts. The divinity, which Mom always made on a clear, cold day so it would not turn sticky, she beat so long and furiously that you could almost imagine sparks jumping from the wire beater as it went clickity-click-click-clickity-click against the sides of the mixing bowl. And the fruit salad must always have three and only three ingredients: California Sunkist oranges, thick slices of fat, solid bananas, and juicy chunks of Dole pineapple. Grapes, peaches, apples, or other fruits were considered "foreign" to real fruit salad. The salad, always stored on the back porch so it would be icy cold, was served with tall, white slices of homemade angel food cake.

There would be other goodies, such as the golden brown baked chicken and crisp cold celery on which Aunt Bertha Anderson prided herself (hers was the brownest chicken and the crispiest celery in Marion). But more sentiment lingers from the moist, white divinity and the cold fruit salad than from anything else.

One explanation for my nostalgia is what happened the Christmas that members of our grade-school band went from house to house playing carols. Our director, George Ashley, suggested that this might be a way to raise money for new uniforms.

Four of us, who played clarinets, were to come to our house. I dreaded to, because Mom and Dad had said that they simply didn't have any cash to give. But we set up our music racks and played "Silent Night" and "O Little Town of Bethlehem." Then Mom went over to the see-through china closet between the kitchen and dining-room and brought out the "depression glass" candy plate, with squares of white and brown and pink candies in each of its sections. Seldom had my friends tasted divinity so smooth and rich, and I will always remember how extravagantly they praised it. Although they were unaware of what it meant to me, what they said eased my boyish embarrassment at being treated with candy instead of money.

If we sent or received Christmas cards, I have no memory of it. Cards and stamps were expendable in the thirties—the few cents they cost were preempted for food and coal and clothing. But there were other ways to show your love.

About December 22, Dad would kill one of his fattest yellow hens. The same morning Mom would dress her, then lay her out on dish cloths to dry. Next the hen was wrapped in white cloths, then in waxed paper or leftover bread wrappers. Finally she went into a box, with wrappings made from paper sacks, and tied with odds and ends of string saved from grocery packages.

Shortly after dinner, Dad would set out for the post office to mail the hen, and the home-baked goodies packed with her in the box, to my sister Afton and her family in St. Louis. We speculated on whether postal regulations permitted uncooked food to be mailed, but we never asked at the window. And the yellow hen was wrapped so securely that no telltale moisture ever leaked through.

So, rather than gifts of clothing or toys, a little chicken that had scratched in the spring grass in a quiet little southern Illinois town found its way to the table of my sister in the city. We sent what we could, and I always sensed that the package was tied by cords of love. Afton often sent us a five-pound box of chocolates for Christmas. There was a special big-city glamor to the chocolate-covered cherries, mints, nougats, caramels, and fudges. We would tuck the box away in the front bedroom, which was closed off in the winter. Here the candy kept cold and firm. Once or twice a day we visited the "big icebox" for a treat, choosing first the pieces wrapped in shiny red or gold. Five pounds of candy lasted way up into January, and we savored every day that Christmas was stretched into the new year.

The one luxury I coveted, Christmas after Christmas, was electric lights for our tree. I often dreamed how wonderful it would be if soft, colored lights could glow among the tattered ornaments we had preserved from the more prosperous twenties.

If I ever want to feel a lump in my throat some dark December day, I relive an afternoon when Mom took me to the Christmas party of her Ladies' Aid, in the home of Mrs. Frank Miles at 1208 North Glendale. Although forty Christmases have come and gone, I can still retrace our steps as we entered a sort of side room or sun porch with several windows, where Mrs. Miles had decorated a fir tree with real electric lights. I recall the sheer ecstasy of lying on the floor, gazing in awe at the lights, so close you could touch them, so near you could feel their tiny warmth.

A big Christmas tree with real lights always stood in the main auditorium of the First Baptist church. And although James Sneddon, the custodian with the Scottish accent, was never known for being stingy when it came to firing the church furnace, there was an emotional warmth that exceeded the eighty degrees on the thermometer. It was the glow of those red, green, and blue Christmas lights.

Many churches no longer erect Christmas trees in their sanctuaries, fearing they are out of harmony with the true meaning of the holiday. But I will always be grateful that someone in my boyhood church took the time to trim and light a big tree whose beauty I could absorb for two or three Sundays each December.

As I walked to church on December evenings, or to a neighbor's, or to town, I picked my route along streets where I could see the most lights. As soon as I passed one house with a lighted tree, I looked for the next one. The windows with Christmas lights formed a bridge for my imagination, a light-strewn path that led me right on to Christmas.

Somehow, one year, I discovered a sixty-watt red light bulb in the house. It gave me an idea. Why not screw the bulb into the overhead socket that hung from the ceiling? It would cast a red glow on the tree, and the reflection on the icicles might look like an actual string of lights. We tried it. Turning out the other lights, Mom, Dad, and I went outside and stood in the winter darkness, right in front of the window where we could see the tree bathed in the soft, red glow of the single overhead bulb.

"Look, it's just like real," I cried excitedly. And for a few moments of imagination we did have a real string of real lights.

Lum and Abner, the popular radio show of the thirties, repeated the same Christmas skit each year. A young couple on their way to the county seat to pay year-end taxes got as far as Pine Ridge, Arkansas, locale of Lum and Abner's Jot-'em-Down store. Here, stopped by a snowstorm, they sought shelter in a nearby barn. The good folks of Pine Ridge, who discovered that the young woman was pregnant, quickly came to their rescue. They arranged for food, blankets, and heat, and then sent for a doctor. On that cold, star-filled night a baby was born.

In the closing episode, Lum and Abner were walking through the snow, carrying a box of home-cooked victuals to the barn. They waxed philosophical as Lum said, "You know, Abner, here we are, two old codgers, our lives about over, and here's this young-un', just comin' into the world . . . sort of like that first Christmas years and years ago. . . ."

As Dad reached over to turn off the Atwater-Kent, he said, "You know, if that wouldn't give a fellow the Christmas spirit, I don't know what could."

No one else said anything. But deep inside, the three of us felt real good, real warm, real Christmassy. And suddenly the lights were shining all over our end of town!

Rockford's First Christmas Tree

ROCKFORD MORNING STAR

As with other communities in Illinois just prior to the Civil War, Rockford was being introduced to the symbols of Christmas that have become familiar to Illinoisans today.

All over our land tonight, thousands of boys and girls are telling the story of the first Christmas tree, which blossomed in all its rare beauty in a cabin in the Black Forest as a reward for the kindness shown by the children of the home for a poor deserted outcast child; and as they tell their tale, let us recall the first Christmas tree that ever delighted the eyes of little ones in this far-away western village—for all the world over the children are blessed by the fruits of these seeds of love sewn by a child centuries ago.

It was Mr. Conant, pastor of the little old Unitarian church which still stands, miserable and neglected, on the corner of Chestnut and South Church Streets, who introduced the Christmas tree to Rockford churches during the holidays of 1857 or 1858. You know our early settlers were largely the descendants of the old New England stock; and the children of those stern men who in 1621 punished all who dared make a holiday of the Christmas day were not likely to give much thought to the celebration of the day. But there were among us a few families of German extraction to whom Santa Claus and his reindeers were veritable realities, and in those parlors the glorious tree blossomed as often as the day came around. Mr. Julius Gerber was one of those, and as the Gerbers and the Conants were close friends, the pastor's great love for children saw in this beautiful custom a new way of bestowing happiness upon the children of his flock.

Draping the Christmas Tree

During the early months of December that year the mothers of the flock had certain tiny parcels of gay pink tarlatan stowed away in the recesses of their work baskets, which were to be made into dainty transparent bags for candy, just as they made them in the Fatherland; and in the sitting room of the Starr home the daughters of the family were busy gilding nuts, according to the same rule. And just before the happy day, the young folks gathered at the Conant home, where great pans of snowy popcorn and glowing ruby cranberries grew into long chains with which to drape the tree.

On Christmas Eve, the regular sociable of the church was held at the parsonage—the comfortable frame house which still stands on the corner of Green and West Streets. Mr. Conant, bubbling over with reflected happiness, greeted every newcomer with the hearty good cheer which made the parsonage a church home, and his wife, in her rare, quiet way, made us all feel the charm of her motherliness and love.

At the proper time the doors of the great parlors were thrown open, and there, in all its beauty, stood our first Christmas tree. There were the rich green branches, twined and draped with the white and crimson, caught up with the gilded nuts and hundreds of twinkling candies. Here and there on the boughs, laden until they dropped, were realistic glass icicles that sparkled in the candlelight, and the dainty tarlatan bags, through which the colored candies gleamed, blossomed here and there. All day long the fathers and mothers of the congregation had been arriving at the parsonage, bringing mysterious packages of sundry sizes and shapes, for you must know that this was the way in which the fruit which grew upon the tree was supplied. There were dolls, and sleds, and skates, and red and striped mittens and the gay "comforters," such as the boys and men wore in those days, perhaps a set or two of furs, and some rings and other articles of jewelry. But the presents of those days were usually simple and likely to express the love of the giver by the comfort which it brought to the recipient. How lovely it was, to be sure! All the lovelier, because to the majority of the children gathered there, this was the first time they had seen a Christmas tree in full bloom.

By and by the jolly Santa Claus began to strip the fruit from the tree and distribute it to the waiting children; then came the bags, and the nuts, and finally, sad to relate, even the popcorn chains were sacrificed, and went the way of all popcorn.

Still Kept as Souvenirs

All this was many years ago, and the church Christmas tree has come to be an old story with us. But the memory of that first experience still remains with us, and so do some of the gifts which the jolly old Santa kept in sacred drawers, and looked at from time to time, and attributed from that tree, and which are ways with a blessed feeling of tenderness, as though a wave of the old-time loving kindness of the pioneer days was enveloping us with its love and happiness.

Can you close your eyes and let memory bring you once more the vision of that simple parlor, and the wonderful tree, and the dear faces, every one illuminated with happiness and love that surrounded it that night? There were the Conants, of course—father, mother, Coretta, John and Naroy; the Starrs, the Wights, the Blinns, the three Cunningham families, the Gerbers, the Melancton Smiths, the Montagues, the Redingtons, the Kilburns, the Fowlers, the Wymans, the Millers, the Hollands, and the Waldos. Not many of the older ones are still with us, and the little ones of that night are staid men and matrons today. But the fruits of love, whose seeds were sown in that little church through the influence of the tree and in many another thoughtful act, have been blossoming and maturing seed for the bettering of the children and for all mankind through all these years. When the Great Reaper measures the grain, the harvest will be a plentiful one.

Some Words for the Lighting of the Christmas Tree in the Auburn, Illinois, Town Square

JOHN KNOEPFLE

The poet describes a familiar sight in town squares
and parks throughout Illinois at Christmastime.

> this tree will be our own
> rising star it will sparkle
> even if there are clouds in the sky
> this soft-needled fir
> glowing with light
> the greens blues reds
> the yellows all
> the good colors these
> tinsel cheers in a dark evening

the winter wearing to that cold
hour when the snow swirls
may hide the solstice
and we will find once more the
vast dark of the first breaking
from which all the light
gleaming in our eyes was drawn

and so for those who will
come by and share these lights
and for those who have
lived here in our time
or back as far as the generations go
and for those who will yet
move here in some other season
of flickering lights
let us ask a blessing
a blessing for all of them
and for ourselves—and everyone

as we stand in the privilege
of this one instant prepared for us
on this small planet
this manger of reflecting light
in the freedom of the heavens

"Santa Marching to Work" (1895), by Edgar Rice Burroughs

*Snow road,
Saline County, by
Charles Hammond*

Christmas Outdoors

Holidays with Feathers
Forty Years of Christmas Bird Counts

JOEL GREENBERG

This noted naturalist explains that not everyone in Illinois remains near the family hearth during the Christmas holidays. People of all faiths embrace the natural world during this solstice season that beckons them into satisfying winter pursuits.

I personally celebrate two traditions of the holiday season. I light the candles of my menorah, but most of my time and energy goes to an event of much more recent vintage, the Christmas Bird Counts. Created by the ornithologist Frank Chapman in 1900, the idea is for groups to record all the birds they encounter within a designated area (today that is a fifteen-mile-diameter circle). Chapman hoped to supplant the Christmas Day bird hunts with this more benign activity. Twenty-five counts from thirteen states and two provinces were submitted that year. During the 2008 season, thousands of observers participated in hundreds of counts spread across the Western Hemisphere and the Pacific islands. The database assembled over that 108-year span represents the largest of any wildlife monitoring project in the world.

My first CBCs were in 1967 when I was thirteen: Evanston North Shore and Waukegan. In 1968, I added Chicago Lakefront to my repertoire. Over the years, I have

Facing page: Snowy cardinal, Galena, by Barbara Baird

been on a number of other counts, including several outside Illinois, but these are the three that I now organize and have rarely missed. (I have skipped Evanston precisely once—in 1970, when my mother took me on my first birding trip to Texas.)

For many years the Evanston CBC was compiled by Jim and Pat Ware. Jim said he did not want his counters to have to take time off in the middle of the day to prepare their casseroles for the dinner afterwards, so the Wares would provide a fine spread of comestibles. Years later my mother hosted it. (If a couple arrived where one party was not a birder, my sister would encourage that person to hang out in the kitchen, "where the sane people are.") After the group had fortified themselves, the countdown ensued. The birds would be called off in rounds, from most common to least. Thus the suspense built as we learned the results. To keep from spilling the birds early, newly arriving parties answer questions of how they did with a coy, "Oh, not bad," or, "We sure didn't see much."

Evanston holds the record for highest species list in northern Illinois, with a tally of ninety-one set in 2001. Waukegan's high count is eighty-seven. For a number of years, we counted only water birds on the Lakefront and therefore never had very high totals. In 1977, my mother and I did the count by ourselves. It was a brutally cold day, and the lake was unfrozen, but covered with an impenetrable layer of fog. Anything smaller than a swan was a challenge to find and identify. That year we totaled nine species; no count south of Yellowknife, Northwest Territories, had fewer.

The lakefront areas of the Evanston and Waukegan count have always been the most coveted, but I have stuck to the less glamorous inland territories. Most of my day is spent walking along streams where open water and vegetation hold the promise of lingering species, most of which are common at other times of the year. (On the shores of Lake Michigan, counters seek rare gulls and waterfowl whose presence in northeastern Illinois is always noteworthy.)

One of my most productive areas in Evanston is the West Fork of the North Branch of the Chicago River between Deerfield Road on the north and Lake Cook on the south. For the past thirty-five years I have walked along the garbage-strewn and overgrown narrow bank sandwiched between fenced-in backyards and the stream. Two thirds of the distance is downstream of the Deerfield Water Treatment Plant, whose discharge keeps the water moving regardless of air temperature. For the first five of those years, the group leader, Richard Horwitz, dropped me off at Deerfield Road, where the available bank was so meager I had to proceed on hands and knees to prevent slipping off into the frozen ditch. Later I made it easier on myself by starting a little farther south, where bipedal movement was viable. As far as I know, no one else birds this ditch, and I do it once a year or occasionally twice if I have time to scout. It has produced some great birds over the years: ruby crowned kinglet, common snipe, blue-winged teal, and brown thrasher.

On the Waukegan count I cover the Des Plaines River from Route 176 on the south to Route 120 on the north. During the late 1970s we would cover stretches of it on foot, and then drive to other access points. In 1981 we found an eastern phoebe, extremely rare in the winter, perched on a branch over the river. This led me to think that since stretches varied in productivity from year to year, we should walk the whole thing. Thus began twenty-six years of the "Death March." Not surprisingly, only a few people accompanied me more than once. (The march has been shortened in recent years, as I have become older and the area less birdy.)

Two extreme experiences stand out. New Year's Eve 1985 produced a blizzard that carpeted the region in deep snow. Three of us began our trudge along the river but soon found that the going was too exhausting to continue. Al Stokie and Dick Young went back the way we had come, while I decided to minimize my efforts by taking a shorter route to the road from where I could more easily reach the car. Unfortunately, between me and my destination was a marsh, whose nature was hidden by snow. Wading through water never bothered me, and even in winter I do not hesitate getting my legs wet up to the knees. So when I broke through the ice, I was not concerned. But I quickly learned that the ice was too thick for me to walk through; I had to raise my leg high enough to stomp down on it, if I were to move forward. The water kept getting deeper, however, and I was no longer able to lift my leg far enough to smash the ice. I was then forced to use my fists for that purpose, pummeling my way through the frozen pond. Eventually, the declivity began to shallow out and I reached the car, although my pants were frozen. To get the sensation, wear cardboard sometime.

Years later, Margo Milde and Caroline Fields had the east side, and I was alone on the west. At one point, Caroline found a winter wren (a bird often missed on local CBCs) and continued on her way as Margo searched for it. A few minutes later Margo began screaming. While looking for the wren, she had slipped on the slick lip of the bank and was waist deep in water. A dog walker also heard the yells and joined the two. Margo could not move laterally because the sediment was too soft; nor could she climb out, even with help, because the shore had been undercut by the current. Eventually, medics arrived to extricate Margo from her predicament and take her to the nearest emergency room, where staff proclaimed her healthy. She was released soon thereafter and went home to change clothes but was back in the field for the last hour of birding.

The Chicago Lakefront count is unique because although based on the fifteen-mile circle, we restrict our coverage to the lakefront and harbors from Montrose on the north to Jackson Park on the south. For the last twenty-five or so years it is held on Christmas Day. (I have joked it is for people without family or friends; and one year we had a total of four participants who were all Jewish.) Some years, it is the only count conducted anywhere on Christmas Day. But there is a strong practical reason to hold the count on Christmas—Lake Shore Drive is never less crowded, nor are lakefront sites more accessible.

There are two things I want to say about Lakefront. First, while bird numbers are not high, we have had some extraordinarily rare finds. Illinois' second ever tufted duck (a straggler from Europe) dozed among a flock of scaup off Navy Pier one day, while a Brewer's sparrow wintered at the Jarvis Bird Sanctuary in Lincoln Park. This is a western species that has been recorded in the state only a few times. Perhaps the most exciting bird was the state's first confirmed ivory gull discovered in 1992 by Kenae Hirabayashi and Al Stokie at Montrose. This species is a denizen of the Arctic pack ice, one that ordinarily subsists on dead seals and whales.

The second noteworthy aspect of the Lakefront CBC is that the media covers it like no other. I suspect it is a combination of December 25 being a slow news day and the seeming weirdness of getting up before dawn to count birds on a holiday that most people spend engaged in warmer, more domestic pursuits. One reporter from WBBM radio calls me almost every year for a summary of our observations. Three years ago my group saw a mockingbird at McCormick Place. The day after he broadcast the story, the *Chicago Sun-Times* called and wound up printing their own piece on our experience. WBEZ read the newspaper account and the public was treated to yet another version.

The paths that I have trod for decades on these counts both connect me to the past and remind me of the transitory nature of things. Companions, whom I haven't seen in years or whose names I have even forgotten, walk with me still. None of the people mentioned in this article any longer accompanies me on Evanston or Waukegan counts (although most still participate in CBCs). Hopefully, the new crop will stick around for awhile.

Sadder really than the loss of friendships, whose limited spans are understood, are the changes to the landscape. Gone are the evergreens on Route 43 north of Route 22 where we sought the tiny saw-whet owls roosting deep within a copse of junipers. For two years on River Road south of Route 120, we encountered Brewer's blackbirds at a horse farm. By the third year, not only were the blackbirds gone but so were the

"Christmas Morning on the Illinois River" (2008), by David Zalaznik

horses and the farm, replaced by a subdivision of large homes. After the loss of his mate, the last ring-necked pheasant in Evanston's count circle hung on for two more years in an ever-shrinking field before he too disappeared. Even the ditch through which the West Fork of the North Branch now flows intersects Lake-Cook Road at a different point than it did when I first crept along its edge. Engineers have moved it to the east.

I too have changed, of course. Almost out of middle age, I find the counts are more physically demanding then they used to be, yet not as exciting (few things are), for most of the possibilities have been realized. And while I can rely on the cadres of birders who cover their areas every year, it seems to take more effort to make sure sites are still accessible to them. For Waukegan now, I have to make prior arrangements with eight different entities, including a naval base, power plant, and college. But, still, there is no denying the adrenalin rush when I hear that first screech owl before dawn, or catch sight of an unexpected species. These are gifts like no other.

Christmas Bird Count

BEN GELMAN

Birding during the Christmas season brings celebrants of the tradition from far reaches of Illinois together. Here Joel Greenberg goes south to join southern Illinois birders at Christmas.

The annual Audubon Society Christmas Bird Count at Crab Orchard National Wildlife Refuge this year involved not just birds that migrated to the area from the north but migrating bird watchers. A group of seven Chicago-area bird watchers joined ten southern Illinois residents in making the Crab Orchard count. Much of the credit for drawing the upstaters to this area must go to John Robinson of the Crab Orchard refuge staff, an ardent bird watcher himself, who invited them to southern Illinois.

But, according to two of the northerners, Joel Greenberg of Mount Prospect and Howie Nielson of Chicago, they had other reasons, too. They said they had heard of the scenic attractions of the area, for one thing, and had toyed with the idea of coming down to visit. For another, they had noticed in the compilation of last year's Christmas count that Crab Orchard and Horseshoe Lake Conservation Area had tied for the highest number of species with ninety each.

Now, while there is a definite scientific value to the annual bird counts, there is also a certain amount of friendly competition. The Union County Conservation Area census and the Horseshoe Lake census annually attract a group of Springfield-area bird watchers, headed by Vernon Kleen of the Illinois Department of Conservation. Kleen feels at home in this area because he took his master's degree in wildlife management from Southern Illinois University at Carbondale. He also supervises the compilation of Christmas Bird Counts in Illinois. So that did it. Here was a chance for a Chicago-area-versus-Springfield-area contest. As the compiler of the Crab Orchard refuge count, I was delighted to have the extra eyes (and telescopes and binoculars) of the Chicago-area group.

The Crab Orchard count was set up on December 17, the first day of the official count period that runs through January 2. As it turned out, that Saturday was mostly sunny, not too cold (twenty through thirty-two degrees) and, best of all, there was hardly any wind. There is nothing that can chill a person through and through more than standing at the edge of a lake in winter, looking through a telescope at ducks a quarter of a mile away—in the face of a stiff north wind.

Well, with the good weather, the help of the expert bird watchers from upstate, and a little good luck in being in the right place to see some of the rare winter birds, we wound up with a list of ninety-five species, tying the record for the Crab Orchard count set in 1975. Topping the list was a Townsend's solitaire, a casual visitor from the Far West. This gray songbird of the thrush family has been seen before in Illinois, but very rarely. It has been known to stray as far east as New York and Newfoundland in the winter months. The bird found during the Crab Orchard count was seen about two miles northeast of the refuge proper, but well within the fifteen-mile-diameter circle authorized for the count.

Also spotted were a flock of double-crested cormorants and a lone pine warbler, both uncommon winter visitors to the area. The Crab Orchard refuge list included twenty-six bald eagles, sixty-five red-tailed hawks, twenty-four kestrels (sparrow hawks), six red-shouldered hawks, five northern harriers (marsh hawks), two sharp-shinned hawks, one Cooper's hawk, and one rough-legged hawk.

Heading the waterfowl count, as usual, were the Canada geese that winter in the area, twenty-eight thousand of them by official refuge aerial count. Also seen were nine snow geese in the white form and seventeen in the white-headed "blue" form.

Other water birds seen included common loon, both pied-billed and horned grebes, green-winged teal, black duck, mallard, pintail, shoveler, gadwall, American wigeon, canvasback, redhead, ring-necked duck, greater scaup, goldeneye, bufflehead, hooded merganser, common merganser, red-breasted merganser, and ruddy duck.

Several members of the party scouted the area before dawn and came up with five great horned owls, one barred owl, and one screech owl.

Most common species of the day was the red-winged blackbird, of which some sixty-one thousand were counted. Also seen were about twenty-one thousand grackles, eleven thousand brown-headed cowbirds, and two thousand starlings.

The largest bird seen was the great blue heron (sixty-three), and the smallest was a single winter wren. Five species of birds were seen in the Crab Orchard refuge count area the same week—but not the same day—as the official count: great egret, oldsquaw, hermit thrush, eared grebe, and pine siskin. They would have pushed the total up to a record one hundred species.

"December Snow on the Branches" (1945), by May Theilgaard Watts

As things turned out, our record-tying ninety-five species probably will be high for the state this year [1983]. The Horseshoe Lake count was held Tuesday and it turned up eighty-four species, including a huge flock of 110,000 Canada geese. The Union County census, which had been scheduled Wednesday, was called off because of icy road conditions.

Star Silver

CARL SANDBURG

The story of Christmas, the poet tells his readers, is set within nature, and its characters embrace the setting.

The silver of one star
Plays cross-lights against pine green.
And the play of this silver
Crosswise against the green
Is an old story . . .
         thousands of years.
And sheep raisers on the hills by night
Watching the wooly four-footed ramblers,
Watching a single silver star—
Why does the story never wear out?

And a baby slung in a feed-box
Back in a barn in a Bethlehem slum,
A baby's first cry mixing with the crunch
Of a mule's teeth on Bethlehem Christmas corn,
Baby fists softer than snowflakes of Norway,
The vagabond mother of Christ
And the vagabond men of wisdom,
All in one barn on a winter night,
And a baby there in swaddling clothes on hay—
Why does the story never wear out?

The sheen of it all
Is a star silver and a pine green
For the heart of a child asking a story,
The red and hungry, red and hankering heart
Calling for cross-lights of silver and green.

SOME WAYS OF WEARING THE SNOW

WHITE PINE

COLORADO SPRUCE

MUGO PINE

NORWAY SPRUCE

HEMLOCK

BUR OAK

HAWTHORN

HIGH-BUSH CRANBERRY

RHODODENDRON

NINEBARK

*"Some Ways of
Wearing the Snow"
(1945), by May
Theilgaard Watts*

They Wear the Snow with a Difference

MAY THEILGAARD WATTS

This naturalist recognizes in these winter scenes the distinctiveness of Illinois plants in winter snow, images that Illinoisans hope to see when they think of Christmas.

Weather is the master of ceremonies under whose showmanship plants take their turn in the spotlight. Each changing mood points out a specialist. The best performer in dew is probably a lupine leaf; in hoar frost, it is ironwood; and in sleet, the beaded curtain of weeping willow twigs. In the wind the best performer is the white pine; but in a breeze it is the trembling aspen, or silver poplar; while the thirsty wind of a summer drought it is cottonwood, making the sound of rain on the roof. The place on which prevailing westerlies write their permanent record most plainly is a row of willows. A slow spring rain makes the best blue-gray setting for the pale yellow hazel catkins, but a fall rain achieves its triumph when it blackens the trunks of red oak in contrast with the brilliance of fall foliage.

But these are passing moods of weather compared to snow. In this winter of much snow we realize that it is well to be surrounded by those good companions that meet the winter with charm, as well as those that offer spring, summer, or fall display.

Among our native trees, perhaps white oak, bur oak, hawthorn, and ironwood hold the snow most pleasingly. These trees are alike in having a tendency to horizontal branching, but each of them has individuality in holding the snow.

The wide-spreading vigor of white oak receives it, like all weather, serenely, effortlessly; and the bulging biceps of the bur oak with its corky twigs and rough bark make the snow seem a sweater pulled carelessly across the shoulders of a fullback between quarters. On the hawthorn the snow is a loosely crocheted shawl of wool, but on the ironwood it is a precise lacework.

The evergreens have distinctive ways with snow. Those flat overlapping shelves mark Colorado spruce, while the next tree proclaims itself Norway spruce by its manner of holding snow on its ridges and letting it slide from pendent twigs. The hemlock accepts it as an unnecessary adjunct to her sufficiency of grace, and lets it slide from relaxed fingertips. White pine turns its needles down like a fringe below the snow, but mugo pine keeps its needles erect, uplifting neat muffins in its fingers.

But for all the beauty of snow on our evergreens we must not let it lie too heavily, or broken branches will mar future formal symmetry. True, in the north woods and on the mountain tops, they bear their snow without man's interference, but how few of them are symmetrical in old age, or need to be. Especially do the saucer-shaped evergreens, such as yew, common juniper, and Pfitzer juniper, need help to prevent breakage.

Some fruits that persist through the winter have interesting ways with the snow. Each brown raceme of ninebarks wears an elf cap. And high-bush cranberry offers brilliant clustered drupes a la mode to any itinerant flock of cedar waxwings, the only birds that seem to appreciate them.

Some Norway maples and box elders hold characteristic snowy knobs along their trunks.

The rhododendron hardly offers a foothold to snow, but it is a good living thermometer for just outside the window to help one decide whether to wear that extra sweater. When each leaf curls back and points straight down, it is best to wear it, and warm mittens, too. But when the leaves rise 20° from the vertical, it is safe to unwind the mufflers. When the leaves rise above 45° from the vertical, waterproof boots will be useful.

Others that refuse to hold the snow are white birches and weeping willows. The white birch does well to eschew this rival that turns the birch's own much-advertised whiteness to pale yellow. But the ragged bark of river birch holds handfuls of it, enhancing its own coppery tones.

Other colors that profit by contrasting with the snow are the red buds of linden, hawthorn, silver maple, and the fruits of many-flowered rose; the brown leaves of white oak and bayberry; the lavender bloom on arching canes of red raspberry; the orange inner bark of hawthorns; the cinnamon bark of Scotch pine branches; and the green twigs of spice bush and sassafras.

PERSONALLY DRAWN FAMILY XMAS CARDS BY ED BURROUGHS
Back when the money was tight

Uncertainty as to the movements of a certain stock has decided Santa Claus to remain where he is for an indefinite period. We are therefore sending you only our best wishes for A Merry Christmas and A Happy New Year

"Treed by a Moose"
(ca. 1909), by Edgar
Rice Burroughs

*Emily Droege of Galva
as a Lucia, Bishop Hill,
by Mike Wendel*

Eating Merrily

From My Kitchen Window, Christmas 1999

DIXIE TERRY

Dixie Terry of Goreville has been publishing recipes throughout her adult life.
Here she records the pressures and the satisfactions of preparing Christmas dinner.

As I watch the squirrels scurrying around our back yard while I wash up a half dozen loaf pans and a stack of breakfast dishes, it's a reminder that like those squirrels, so many of us are also scurrying.

This is the season to scurry, hurry, and worry, as we attempt to crowd forty-eight hours worth of projects into each twenty-four-hour day.

Why do we think "because it's Christmas!" that we can fit all these extra activities in, when at all other times of the year we can't find time to have parties, go to extra events, do more shopping, cook and bake everything homemade-from-scratch? Our homes are never picture-perfect, so why do we knock ourselves out at holiday time, trying to make our humble abode look like a magazine picture?

Why do we attempt all these extra activities every year in an effort to have a perfect Christmas?

We totally exhaust ourselves in a futile try to have everything in our house to perfection, as the candles glow and the firewood crackles, while a perfectly decorated tree

Facing page: Table at the David Davis Mansion set for Christmas dinner, by Ken Kashian

stands tall and straight nearby. But it just isn't possible to have perfection in a house where people live. And isn't that the purpose of a home—a place for people to gather for comfort and companionship and to share food?

The mantle may be dusty and the stockings hung slightly askew, but does it really matter? Or the fact that your cookies are made from a mix, or that the kitchen floor has not been shined?

As the candles burn brightly and the fireplace roars, what really matters is the togetherness of the season and the welcome feeling offered to guests and family. Whether the food is made from scratch or picked up at a supermarket deli won't be remembered, but the love and warmth in the manner it's served up will be a long-remembered part of life.

As we remember why we celebrate Christmas, maybe it can be simplified this year, as we head into the new millennium. Maybe we can relax our expectations a bit and enjoy life for what it is, a celebration of each hour, as it occurs.

No time for extra baking? Maybe one or two of these easy-do recipes can be put together in your kitchen some evening after supper.

I plan to light the candles, turn on a program of Christmas carols for a bit of holiday joy as I stir up a bounty of cookies that are good for giving.

Candied Fruit Cookies

1 cup butter	2 cups uncooked oats
1 cup sugar	¾ teaspoon cinnamon
2 eggs	1 teaspoon salt
½ cup milk	½ teaspoon nutmeg
2 cups plus 1 tablespoon flour	½ cup nuts
½ teaspoon baking soda	1 cup candied fruit

Combine all ingredients in order. Reserve ½ cup flour to be mixed with fruit before adding it. Drop by rounded teaspoons on ungreased baking sheet. Bake for 11 minutes at 375°

Maple Pecan Squares

CRUST:

1½ cups flour
¼ cup brown sugar

½ cup butter, soft

FILLING:

⅔ cup brown sugar
1 cup maple syrup
2 eggs, beaten
2 tablespoons flour

¼ teaspoon salt
½ teaspoon vanilla
1 cup pecans, chopped

Combine crust ingredients with a fork until consistency of fine corn meal. Press mixture into ungreased 9x13–inch baking pan. Bake at 350° for 15 minutes. Combine brown sugar and syrup in small saucepan and simmer 5 minutes. Pour over beaten eggs, stirring constantly. Stir in remaining ingredients except nuts. Pour mixture over baked crust; sprinkle with nuts and bake at 350° for 20 to 25 minutes. Cool in pan. Cut in bars.

Orange Crispies

1¼ cups 40% Bran Flakes
1¼ cups sifted flour
1 teaspoon baking powder
½ teaspoon salt
1½ teaspoons grated orange rind

½ cup butter or butter-flavored shortening
1 cup sugar
1 egg
1 tablespoon milk
1 tablespoon orange juice

Crush cereal. Sift together flour, baking powder, and salt. Cream orange rind, shortening and sugar together until mixture is light and fluffy. Add egg and beat thoroughly. Then blend in milk and orange juice. Add flour mixture gradually, blending well. Stir in cereal. Chill until firm enough to roll. Roll ⅛ inch thick on lightly floured board. Cut with floured 2 ½-inch cookie cutter. Bake on greased baking sheet in hot oven (425°) for 6–8 minutes. Decorate cookies with frosting and sprinkles or nuts, if desired. Makes 3–4 dozen.

Crunchy Fudge Sandwiches

6-ounce package butterscotch morsels
½ cup peanut butter
4 cups Rice Krispies
6-ounce package semisweet
  chocolate morsels

½ cup sifted powdered sugar
2 teaspoons butter
1 tablespoon water

Melt butterscotch morsels with peanut butter in heavy saucepan over low heat, stirring until blended. Stir in Rice Krispies. Press half of the mixture into buttered 8-inch square baking pan. Chill. Set remainder aside. Stir over hot water semisweet chocolate morsels and powdered sugar. Add 2 teaspoons butter and 1 tablespoon water and stir until chocolate is melted. Spread over chilled mixture. Top with reserved mixture. Chill again.

Double Chocolate Crumble Bars

½ cup butter
¾ cup sugar
2 eggs
1 teaspoon vanilla flavoring
¾ cup flour

½ cup chopped pecans
2 tablespoons baking cocoa
¼ teaspoon baking powder
¼ teaspoon salt

TOPPING:

2 cups miniature marshmallows
1 6-ounce package semisweet
  chocolate chips

1 cup creamy peanut butter
1½ cups crisp rice cereal

Cream butter and sugar; beat in eggs and vanilla. Set aside. Stir together flour, chopped nuts, cocoa, baking powder and salt; stir into egg mixture. Spread in bottom of greased

13x9–inch baking pan. Bake at 350° for 15–20 minutes or until bars test done. Sprinkle marshmallows evenly on top; bake 3 minutes more. Cool. In small saucepan, combine chocolate chips and peanut butter; cook and stir over low heat until chocolate is melted. Stir in cereal. Spread mixture on top of cooled bars. Chill; cut in 3–4 dozen bars.

Cream Cheese Cookies

½ cup butter
1 3-ounce package cream cheese
½ cup sugar
¼ teaspoon almond extract

1 cup flour
2 teaspoons baking powder
¼ teaspoon salt
3½ cups crushed Wheaties cereal

Cream first four ingredients. Stir in dry ingredients. Chill 1–2 hours. Shape into balls and roll in Wheaties. Bake at 350° for 12–15 minutes. Makes 2 ½ dozen.

Christmas Joys

4 tablespoons butter
3 cups powdered sugar
6 tablespoons cream of coconut

4 cups coconut
8 ounces semisweet chocolate chips
unsalted almonds

Cream butter, sugar and cream of coconut together. Mix in coconut. Form balls around an unsalted almond. Dip each ball, using toothpicks, into melted chocolate mixture of semisweet chocolate chips, thinned with small chunks of paraffin. Keep chocolate mix warm while dipping the balls. Place on waxed paper.

Lebkuchen

½ cup honey
½ cup molasses
¾ cup brown sugar, packed
1 egg
1 tablespoon lemon juice
1 teaspoon grated lemon rind
2 ¾ cups flour

½ teaspoon baking soda
1 teaspoon cinnamon
1 teaspoon cloves
1 teaspoon allspice
1 teaspoon nutmeg
⅓ cup cut-up citron
⅓ cup chopped nuts

Mix honey and molasses; bring to a boil. Stir in sugar, egg, lemon juice and rind. Measure flour and sift with dry ingredients; mix in citron and nuts. Chill overnight. Heat oven to 400°. Roll small amount at a time, keeping the rest of the dough chilled. Roll ¼ inch thick; cut into oblongs 2 ½ x 1½ inches. Place 1 inch apart on a greased baking sheet. Bake 10–12 minutes or until no imprint remains when touched lightly. While cookies bake, make glazing icing: Boil together 1 cup sugar and ½ cup water until it forms a thread when a spoon is dipped in and held up. Stir in ¼ cup powdered sugar and brush hot icing lightly over cookies. If icing gets sugary, reheat slightly, adding a little water until clear again. Makes 6 dozen 3x2–inch cookies.

Gingies

⅓ cup soft shortening
1 cup brown sugar, packed
1½ cups dark molasses
⅔ cup cold water
6 cups flour
2 teaspoons baking soda

1 teaspoon salt
1 teaspoon allspice
1 teaspoon ginger
1 teaspoon cloves
1 teaspoon cinnamon

Mix shortening, brown sugar and molasses thoroughly. Stir in water. Sift flour with other dry ingredients. Mix with other mixture. Chill. Heat oven to 350°. Roll dough ½-inch thick. Cut with 2 ½-inch round cookie cutter. Place far apart on lightly greased baking sheet. Bake about 15 minutes or until no imprint remains when touched lightly. Frost cooled cookies with easy cream icing: Blend 1 cup sifted powdered sugar, ¼ teaspoon salt and ½ teaspoon vanilla or other flavoring, such as lemon, almond, or peppermint. Add enough liquid to make it easy to spread, about 1 tablespoon water or 1½ tablespoons milk or cream. Tint, if desired, with a few drops of food coloring. Spread on cookies with spatula or pastry brush.

Old-Time Recipes

LAURA H. HOLMAN

Wild game once provided the meat for Christmas dinners, and it came with special accompaniments. In his Outdoor Illinois *magazine, Dan Malkovich (yes, the father of John) published these recipes by a Benton author of six books of recipes.*

Venison with Sour Cream

2 lbs. venison

1 cup sour cream

¼ cup fat

1 clove garlic

1 cup diced celery

1 cup diced carrots

½ cup minced onion

2 cups water

1 bay leaf

1 teaspoon salt

4 tablespoons butter

4 tablespoons flour

1 cup flour

Cut venison in pieces and melt fat in heavy frying pan or iron skillet. Add meat and garlic, brown on all sides and arrange in a dish.

Put vegetables in remaining fat and cook for two minutes. Add salt, pepper and water. Pour over meat and bake in slow oven until meat is tender.

Melt butter in skillet and stir in flour. Add water in which the meat was cooked and boil until thick. Add sour cream and more salt, if necessary. Pour over meat and vegetables; serve with buttered noodles and currant or mint jelly.

This is an old and excellent way to prepare the deer meat brought home by your hunter.

Larded Grouse

grouse	melted butter
bacon	flour
water	

On each bird lay thin slices of bacon until bird is completely covered. Wrap with string to keep bacon in place. Put in roasting pan and pour over birds sufficient water to provide basting. Roast for 20–25 minutes at 400°.

Remove strips of bacon, brush birds with melted butter, dredge with flour and place in oven again until birds turn a rich golden brown.

Lemon Dumplings

baking powder biscuit dough	butter
¾ cup sugar	flour
1 lemon	boiling water

Make rich baking powder biscuit dough. Pat it into shape and cut small biscuits from it.

Preheat oven to 400°.

Place in bottom of a pan sugar, rind and juice of lemon, and dots of butter. Cover with a sprinkling of flour. Place the biscuits on top of this so they just miss touching each other.

Pour boiling water gently between them as they are in the pan until they are about half covered. Bake until done.

The water and seasonings make the sauce to go with the dumplings.

Roasted Wild Duck

Clean, wipe and dry the ducks. Sprinkle generously with flour, salt and pepper.

Place whole peeled onion inside each duck and place them in self-basting roaster. Fasten with toothpicks two or three strips of bacon across each bird, if desired.

Ducks may be stuffed with wild-rice dressing made by boiling wild rice, seasoning salt, pepper and chopped onion.

Cover bottom of roaster with water. Cover tightly and roast in oven at 350° for 1½ to two hours, depending upon the number and size of the ducks.

Remove cover of the roaster for the last 15 or 20 minutes, to allow skin to brown.

Traditional Egg Nog

3 eggs, separated
dash of salt
3 tablespoons sugar
1¼ cup milk (sweet)

¾ teaspoon vanilla
1 cup sweet cream
nutmeg or grated orange rind

Put the yolks in a bowl and set bowl in a pan of cracked ice. Add salt and heat well. Add sugar and continue heating until well blended. Add the milk and vanilla and mix thoroughly. Pour mixture into punch bowl. When ready to serve, add the cream and fold in the egg whites, beaten stiff but not dry.

Sprinkle with grated nutmeg or grated orange rind and serve.

You may chill in refrigerator if desired.

Candied Sweet Potatoes

6 medium-size sweet potatoes
½ cup white corn syrup
½ cup sugar

1 teaspoon salt
4 tablespoons butter

Parboil sweet potatoes in boiling water (with skins on). Cool and remove skins. Cut potatoes in half, lengthwise.

Put in a greased baking dish. Then boil corn syrup, sugar, salt and butter until thick, pour over sweet potatoes and bake at 350° for one hour. Turn sweet potatoes over occasionally.

Christmas Peanut Brittle

2 cups sugar

1 teaspoon vanilla

1 cup white corn syrup

3 cups raw or fresh roasted peanuts

½ cup water

1 tablespoon butter

½ teaspoon soda

Cook sugar and syrup to soft ball stage. Add butter and peanuts and cook until syrup will spin a long, brittle thread when dropped from a spoon, or until very brittle when dropped into cold water.

Remove from heat and add vanilla and baking soda. Stir until foaming stops.

Pour into greased pans and spread very, very thinly; let cool, then break in pieces.

Christmas Stuffing, Cookies, and Klaben
Hegeler Carus Family Recipes

ELISABETH S. CARUS

For over a century, the Hegeler Carus Mansion in LaSalle has been associated with Open Court Publishing, one of the earliest and most important publishers of philosophical, scientific, and religious writings in the country. Members of the family lived there from 1876 to 2004, and Christmas recipes have been passed down from generation to generation. Edward Hegeler (1835–1910) and his wife Camilla Weisbach Hegeler (1835–1908) came to Illinois from Germany prior to the Civil

War. They both had an interest in food that was passed down to their daughter, Mary Hegeler Carus (1861–1936), and to her children Edward (Elisabeth Carus's grandfather, 1890–1975), Gustave (1892–1960), Mary Elisabeth (Libby, 1896–1990), Paula (1894–1954), Herman (1899–1993), and Alwin (1901–2004).

Turkey Stuffing

According to Aunt Libby, Uncle Alwin, and Uncle Herman, it was traditional to have a different stuffing for each cavity of the turkey. I vaguely remember that it was an oyster stuffing for the larger cavity (which led to a discussion about how oysters were brought to the Midwest in the 1800s).

I was told this recipe came from Camilla Hegeler. Depending upon your taste, you used either wine or brandy. When we were discussing this recipe (from memory only) there was a big debate about which alcohol should be used, but the copy I found in Mary Hegeler's notes indicated it could be either one.

3–5 eggs, separated
1 cup butter
4 ounces sugar
salt to taste
2 ounces citron

1 ounce currants or seedless raisins
¼ teaspoon or more mace
½ pound fresh bread crumbs
2 shot glasses wine or brandy (3–4 ounces)

Beat egg yolk, and whip egg whites. Cream butter, add beaten yolk. Blend well. Add sugar and again beat well. Add salt, citron, currants (or raisins) and mace. Moisten bread crumbs with brandy or wine, then add to creamed mixture. Fold in whipped egg whites. Stuff the crop (i.e. small opening) of the turkey.

Platzchen

This was a year-round favorite. Mr. Hegeler considered this a healthy recipe to give the children since it did not have a lot of ingredients that he considered unhealthy.

For example, he would not allow baking powder. Uncle Alwin indicated that this was included in the cookie selection at Christmas time. It has a nice chewy texture and a delicate flavor. I have never found this exact recipe in any other cookbook. The closest I have found is one that is let to sit overnight and has more ingredients.

4 eggs	1 cup white sugar
2 cups flour	1 teaspoon finely ground anise seeds*

Use parchment paper or beeswax.† Stir the eggs until lemon color. Stir in the sugar. Add flour. Add ground anise seed. Sprinkle whole anise seeds on the baking tray and drop about 1 tablespoon of dough onto the baking pan for each cookie. Bake [at 350°] until done (which is when they are a pale brown on top and a medium brown on the bottom).

---

* 1 tsp pounded into a fine grind (Aunt Libby used a mortar and pestle), then sifted with a small strainer, plus whole seeds to sprinkle on the baking pan under the cookies. I have successfully substituted anise flavoring for the ground anise when I was not able to grind the seeds.

† Beeswax can be found in chunks from beekeepers. You place the baking pan on the stove over a flame to heat up the pan. Take a piece of beeswax and carefully move the wax so a thin layer is melted over the entire pan. Using wax makes a nice smooth bottom that is not greasy. Parchment paper is an acceptable substitute. Using oil will give a different texture to the bottom of the cookie. In my 1946 edition of *The Joy of Cooking*, Irma Rombauer also recommends using beeswax when baking cookies. Mary Hegeler Carus and Irma Rombauer were friends, and Aunt Paula was a friend of Mrs. Rombauer's daughter Marion Rombauer Becker.

Springerle

This was one of four Christmas cookies (Springerle, S cookies, Pfferfernusse, and cinnamon stars) that Aunt Libby made every year. It was fun to use all the different molds (which need to be smooth and deeply enough cut so the imprint will stay—some of the cheaper molds are too shallow). The family molds included a large Santa Claus, very small (1 inch) ones, and round flowered ones. I preferred using beeswax on the pan—it gives a smooth and brown bottom to the cookie. Aunt Libby always used the hartshorn for this recipe, although her mother (Mary Hegeler Carus) indicated in her handwritten notes that this was optional. This cookie can be either soft or hard. Mary Hegeler Carus and Aunt Libby liked them hard. My grandmother (Dorothy Carus, 1895–1985) preferred them soft.

1 pound powdered sugar	1 lemon peel
4 to 5 eggs	juice ½ lemon
1 pound flour	1 tablespoon hartshorn*
	(ammonium bicarbonate), optional

Stir sugar into eggs slowly. Add flour, lemon peel, lemon juice and hartshorn. Beat by hand ¾ hour if not using hartshorn.† Let dough stand 4 hours. Prepare baking pans using butter, parchment paper, or coat with beeswax. (See platzchen recipe for directions on using beeswax.) Sprinkle with anise seed. Roll out the dough about ¼ inch. Coat the molds with powdered sugar and press into the dough. Cut out the cookies and place on prepared baking pans. Let cookies dry overnight and bake at 350° until lightly browned on top and medium brown on the bottom.

---

*Hartshorn can usually be found at pharmacies in Italian or Scandinavian neighborhoods, at Italian grocery stores, or by mail order from www.KingArthurFlour.com.
† Using hartshorn will reduce the beating time and make the cookie crisper.
Note: These cookies are best made several weeks ahead and kept in a tin.

Bremen Klaben

Thanks to my sister, Kate Carus, we have the directions for this recipe, since she spent a lot of time with Aunt Libby to learn how to make it. It is an old recipe [which came from the Hegeler family] and was a favorite. As you can see, it is a lot of work to make; so Aunt Libby didn't make it very often as she got older, especially since it was possible to mail order a decent klaben.

Grated lemon peel from 1 lemon	3 pounds flour (12 cups)
2 pounds currants	8 teaspoons cinnamon
1½ pounds raisins	3 teaspoons cardamon

8 ounces chopped citron

8 ounces almonds, ground

3 envelopes [7 teaspoons] dry yeast

½ pounds sugar (divided)

1 quart milk (divided)

2 teaspoons nutmeg

1¼ pounds of butter

1 tablespoon vegetable oil

2 egg yolks and 1 teaspoon water

In a large bowl mix fruits and almonds and set aside. In a small bowl mix yeast, 3 teaspoons sugar, and ¾ cup warm milk. Let stand 5 minutes. In a very large bowl add spices, butter, and remaining sugar to remaining milk. Add yeast mixture and half the flour. Keep adding flour until you have a soft dough. Place remaining flour on board or counter top then knead dough on floured countertop until smooth and elastic.

Place dough into greased bowl. Turn over so greased side is on top. Cover with a cloth and let rise until double in bulk. Punch down and knead in ⅔ of the fruit. Cut into 4 equal pieces. Form dough into crescents on greased baking sheets. Make a long indentation in the center of each crescent. Add the remaining fruit to the indentations then cover with dough on the sides. Let rise until double in bulk. Brush top with egg yolk and water mixture. Bake in 375° oven for 45 minutes.

Per notes from Mary Hegeler Carus, you can make the following modifications:

Fruit: can also add candied pineapple, candied cherries, or sultanas (dried Thompson Seedless grapes) with fruit. Mary Hegeler Carus also showed a larger amount of fruit.

Lemon peel: can use rose water, orange flower water, lemon oil, orange oil or grated orange peel instead of lemon peel.

Spices: can also add mace and cloves.

Collinsville's Queen of Cookies

HERMILDA LISTEMAN

The late Hermilda Listeman of Collinsville delighted in presenting holiday visitors with platters heaped high with cookies baked from recipes in her vast cookbook library. Listeman's cookbook and cookery collection, numbering over three thousand items, is a part of the University of Illinois at Urbana-Champaign library. Her cousin by marriage, May Berenbaum of Urbana, selected the following recipes—all "Herm" originals—for Christmas in Illinois.

Ginger Snaps

"I worked several recipes and then got the flavor I wanted."

¾ cup butter

2 cups sugar and sugar for tops

2 eggs

½ cup molasses

2 teaspoons vinegar

1 teaspoon vanilla

3¾ cups flour

1½ teaspoons soda

2 teaspoons ginger

½ teaspoon cinnamon

¼ teaspoon cloves

Preheat oven to 325°. Cream butter and sugar. Beat the eggs and stir them into the butter- sugar mix, along with the molasses, vinegar, and vanilla. Sift and add the dry ingredients. Mix until blended. Refrigerate the dough for about an hour.

Form dough into ¾ inch balls. Dip tops with finger in water and then into regular sugar.

Bake on greased cookie sheet about 12 minutes.

Yugoslav Nut Crescents

"My mom's [recipe]. These were Christmas favorites. Don't make too big."

1 cup butter

½ cup granulated sugar

1 teaspoon vanilla

2 cups flour

⅓ cup ground walnuts

sifted powered sugar

Preheat oven to 325°. Cream butter, granulated sugar, and vanilla. Stir in flour and walnuts. Shape into crescents. Place on ungreased baking sheet. Bake for 20 minutes. While cookies are slightly warm, roll in powdered sugar.

Chocolate Surprises

"These are a must at Christmas. Very, very good and different from vanilla wafer balls."

1 (6-ounce) package semisweet chocolate morsels	⅛ pound (½ stick) butter
½ cup dairy sour cream	¼ cup cocoa or ground chocolate
dash salt	1 cup confectioners sugar
2 cups vanilla-wafer crumbs	1 cup finely chopped pecans or walnuts
¼ cup rum	¼ teaspoon salt
	cocoa or chocolate sprinkles

Melt chocolate morsels over hot water. Remove from heat and stir in sour cream and dash salt. Chill in refrigerator overnight.

Next day, roll vanilla wafers with a rolling pin to make fine crumbs. Mix crumbs with rum, melted butter, cocoa, confectioners sugar, nuts, and salt with fork or fingertips until mixture holds a shape easily.

Form chilled chocolate mixture into grape-sized balls. Now cover the chocolate center (this is the surprise) with the vanilla wafer crumb mixture. At this point they are the size of walnuts. Roll in additional cocoa and refrigerate in airtight container for 24 hours to mellow. The rum flavor is accented with cold storage.

Makes 2 ½ dozen.

Thumb Print Cookies

"This makes a very pretty cookie and tastes good!"

1 cup butter
⅔ cup sugar
1 egg
2½ cups sifted flour

½ teaspoon salt
1 teaspoon vanilla
white of 1 egg, slightly beaten
1 cup finely chopped nuts

Cream butter and sugar. Beat in egg. Combine and add flour, salt, and vanilla. Chill dough 3 to 4 hours.

Preheat oven to 375°. Pinch off pieces of dough and roll in 1-inch balls. Roll balls in egg white, then roll in nuts.

Bake for 5 minutes at 375°. Press the center of each cookie. Continue baking until done, about 8 minutes. When cool, fill pits with jelly, jam, icing, or cherry, etc.

Black Walnut Drops

"Another favorite cookie if you like black walnuts. A nice cookie to add to an assortment. I always made [these] for Christmas."

½ cup shortening or lard
⅓ cup butter
¼ cup powdered sugar
1 teaspoon vanilla

1 tablespoon milk
2 cups flour
1 teaspoon baking soda
2 cups black walnuts, coarsely chopped

Cream shortening and butter. Add powdered sugar and cream until light. Add vanilla and milk and continue creaming until well blended. Sift together flour and baking soda. Add flour mixture gradually, blending well. Add walnuts.

Roll lightly into balls the size of hickory nuts. Bake in 325° oven 30 minutes or until light brown. Roll in powdered sugar when cooled.

Makes 5 dozen.

Noisy Cookies and Pickled Smelt/Herring

MARJORIE ABRATH SNYDER

The history of Chicago's ever-changing neighborhoods reflects the diversity of cultures that make up Illinois. During the Christmas holidays, these differences offer a chance to share traditions with others. Marjorie Abrath Snyder is co-author of The Wisconsin Herb Cookbook *and* The Michigan Herb Cookbook.

I grew up in Chicago in an Italian neighborhood. As a first-generation German-American, I was a little uncomfortable with how I fit in, particularly during the holidays. But as long as the traditions featured food, there was no problem. Christmas at our house started on December 6—Kris Kringle Day. My father, a native of Essen, Germany, did a fair amount of our family's cooking, relying on his father's pretty well-used cookbook written in German. Opa (my grandfather) had owned a hunting lodge frequented by Kaiser Wilhelm and his friends. The bounty of their hunts was cooked for them by Opa, who also served as chef. Our Christmas dinner was from the cookbook, which I still have, including things like goose and pheasant—coincidentally a northern Italian specialty. One of my Dad's favorite holiday recipes was Opa's famous Christmas cookies. They were called Speculace—a crisp, sugar cookie that my brother and I nicknamed "noisy" cookies because they were so hard and crisp that when you ate them you couldn't hear what people were saying. They were so delicious.

Making them was a marathon event lasting several weeks. Dad would take out his trusty gram scale, also from Germany, and would carefully weigh all the ingredients, even the eggs. Everything was mixed on the table—no bowls. He mixed the lemony dough with his bare hands, and my brother and I would always ask if he had washed them first. He'd look up, smile, and say, "No, but they're clean now." Then the dough had to rest for several days in the refrigerator to develop the cinnamon and lemon flavors.

Finally, the fun part started for us kids. My mother would roll out the cookies, and we'd cut out Christmas trees, stars, Santas, reindeer, and every once in a while we'd sneak a taste of the yummy raw dough. In those days there wasn't the fear of salmonella or other food bacteria. Why, my mother even left the butter out for days at a time! After the cookies were decorated and baked, they were placed in metal cookie tins and stored for a few more weeks to "cure." Of course, we couldn't wait that long, so many of them were gone by Christmas Eve. We discovered that the longer they cured, the better they tasted and the "noisier" they were. To this day, a Christmas isn't complete unless one of the men in the family makes at least one batch of those wonderful "noisy" cookies and mixes the ingredients on the table!

Opa's Speculaci

4 cups flour
2 cups sugar
½ pound butter, softened

3 eggs
2 teaspoons ground cinnamon
1 tablespoon freshly grated lemon rind

Mix half the flour and half the sugar. Cut in butter until crumbly. Add eggs, one at a time, and mix well after each. Alternate rest of flour and sugar. Blend in cinnamon and lemon rind and mix into a flat round. Cover with plastic and refrigerate 2–3 days.

Roll out on a lightly floured surface ¼–½" thick and cut out cookies. Place on greased baking sheets. Brush cookies with egg wash (one beaten egg white) and sprinkle on colored sugar. Bake at 350° until lightly golden, about 15 minutes. Cool on racks then place in cookie tins and "cure" for several weeks.

Besides cookies, my dad used his trusted cookbook to make another holiday favorite— pickled herring, though in Lake Michigan, he had to settle for smelt. In the spring, he would catch the fish himself somewhere off the piers between Oak Street and North Avenue. I don't recall how long he would be out fishing, but when he came home he would have nearly a bushel of the silvery fish. Then he'd go down to the basement and make a brine of salt, vinegar, water, and whole cloves. He'd cut up the fish, skin still on, and layer them in a large wooden barrel. It seemed like that barrel smell was in the basement for months. And only on Christmas Eve were we allowed to enjoy its contents. Usually we ate the herring/smelt with hearty pumpernickel bread and pickled beets, and if my Dad was really ambitious, he'd make Opa's boiled potato, pickled beet, and pickled herring salad. I don't know what it was called, but we thought it was awful. Why ruin three perfectly fine foods by combining them? Today I'm the only one left in the family who enjoys pickled herring, but I don't make it the old-fashioned way. I just buy it from the grocery store like everyone else.

Christmas Dinner without End, Amen

DEAN YANNIAS

The author, a professional writer living now in Oak Park, captures an experience many Illinoisans lucky enough to have lived in the same neighborhood with two grandmothers—let alone Greek grandmothers—have had at Christmas.

According to my two ancient widowed Greek grandmothers who wielded limitless power, our family's Christmas celebrations—the commercialized version of postwar *American* Christmas—bordered on the apostate. But for the dinners they served, these matriarchs did not approve of excess.

They smiled benignly as we opened our presents, but they shared little of our excitement. What were these things that signified Christmas? their smiling indulgent silence seemed to ask. A dwarfish pine tree set in a corner? Glittering wasteful and dangerous electric lights? Arrogantly fragile glass ornaments? The endless parade of gifts? Such a wealth of excess only reminded them of the hard lean years when they struggled to feed their children. This American Christmas tempted fate, invited the Evil Eye to cast malice their way, to hurl misfortune on them and their families, to nullify their current though always evanescent state of grace. Celebrating *American* Christmas was asking for wholesale trouble.

Within the sprawling grid of Chicago, there are indistinct areas Chicagoans refer to as being "near the Loop" (the heart of mid-city) or "far" (lining the city's boundaries). A line drawn due west from the Loop to the first western suburb extends about eight miles. Divide the line in half and you're on the West Side. I grew up in Humboldt Park, *the* West Side. Not the Near West Side or Far West Side, but *the* West Side. It's where we lived, a small gathering of Greeks, West Side Greeks. (Catholics subdivided the city differently, by parish: St. Ann's, St. Leo's, St. Boniface. The rest of us used the compass, adding *Near* and *Far* as needed.)

Midway through World War II, and within months of each other, the two women who would become my grandmothers were elevated to the status of the Greek Widow. They buried their husbands in a then-distant country cemetery—which is now in the Chicago suburb of River Grove. My grandfathers, best friends in life, died not knowing that one's son would marry his best friend's daughter. "Of course they know. Death isn't ignorance," which is more or less what both my grandmothers told me when I was old enough to ask such a question.

Born just before the war's end, I was named at my baptism after my father's father, the same name as my mother's father. Constantine. "A convenient compromise" was the family joke. In the Greek tradition, male children are named after their fraternal grandfather, and we are all named after the saints: Nicholas, Andrew, Anne, Peter, Philip, Agnes—only five dozen options in all, so there's a high probability of duplication. (Birthdays are secondary to "name's days"—another perverse religious homage to ancient custom. A birthday anniversary is to *American* Christmas as a name's day is to Easter.)

My grandmothers were cordial but not outwardly affectionate toward each other. Friendly, but of different temperatures of friendship. On Sunday, they attended the Assumption, the West Side Chicago Greek Orthodox church, greeting each other with respectable affection and decorum, but seldom sitting together. I don't know why. They rarely visited, although they lived, with their few unmarried children, with less than a mile separating their second-floor apartments. "I would like to visit with her, but her stairs are *so* steep"—the excuse they both gave when asked, as if by mutual agreement. They never telephoned each other. When the phone rang, someone else answered it. It was too foreign, too dangerous for them to touch. The telephone possessed invisible, fearful power and was a harbinger of death and bad news.

They'd been wives and mothers and now were hobbling widows with grandchildren. Cloistered within the solid enclave of West Side Greeks, these superstitious, hard-minded, lovely old women worshiped their children and their children's offspring with a widowed matriarch's tribal ferocity.

My father's mother lavished us with Oreos (a Greek word, by the way, meaning "wonderful") when we visited: I called her Yaya Cookie. The name stuck. On the upright piano at my mother's mother's house perched a mounted pheasant, shot in the

1920s by her husband's second cousin who lived in Crystal Lake. Its piercing glass eyes and sharp beak terrorized me. I named her Yaya Baboo , Grandmother Bird.

For Yaya Cookie and Yaya Baboo, food was sacred, a divine gift. Every one of their children, my many aunts and uncles, survived the 1930s in a desperate Chicago. Every meal was a gift from God, and every morsel the Eucharist. The food they cooked kept their children healthy; it meant life. Plump children often survived; thin ones wasted away. "Eat!" meant "breathe!" meant "live!" Their food was sign and substance of their fierce love—ancient, holy Greek medicine for life.

But for us, the grandchildren, each of my grandmothers prepared a huge Christmas dinner served barely three hours apart: two Christmas dinners on Christmas Day, an abundance of love. A dual feast. And—by God!—both Christmas dinners would be eaten. Every bite. Two Christmas dinners consumed with obvious and open joy, or we, the ingrate grandchildren, simply didn't love our grandmothers. Who could resist a grandmother's expression of love? Especially the love of two old grandmothers who couldn't speak English, who couldn't read English or Greek, who never dialed a phone, who never rode on a streetcar?

On Christmas morning, in our two-flat home on the West Side, my brothers and I ripped through the glittering pile of presents under our tree. After breakfast, we all knew it was time. So we dressed in our best clothes and waded through the snow to the round-fendered Oldsmobile for the trip to Yaya Baboo's. For Christmas dinner number one.

Turkey is an American bird. It's not a traditional Greek dish, just a fancy chicken. We knew that turkeys were cooking at each house—stuffed with steaming rice dressing made of sweet tomato sauce, spiced with cinnamon, festooned with roasted chestnuts, garnished with raisins and celery, and all baked with butter and turkey fat. A huge salad of tomatoes and cucumbers (from old-man Fefelis's greenhouse, a converted garage nearby, a trusted source of winter vegetables), onions, feta cheese, olives. Trays of sweet potatoes, mashed, drowned in butter and sprinkled with brown sugar. Mountains of bread. Mounds of mashed white potatoes. Soggy green beans and corn and tart cranberry sauce from cans. Our heaping plates suddenly appeared. I recited grace in Greek and was praised. Christmas dinner number one had begun, and we commenced to eat.

And we ate until our plates were clean, and after they'd been refilled, we ate more. We then assaulted the desserts. Baklava, crumbly Christmas cookies dusted in powdered sugar, rice pudding, glasses of milk. Dazed with food and more food, my brothers and I stumbled from the table into the front room, where under a modest Christmas tree we found more presents, practical clothes for growing children.

"A Guide to Citizens,"
by Art Geisert

Then, only midway through the stupor of our early Christmas afternoon, we bundled up for the short ride through the snow to Yaya Cookie's for Christmas dinner number two—a near duplicate of dinner number one both in terms of volume and menu selection. We ate it all, of course. Second helpings too. More turkey. More sweet potatoes. More corn and beans. More bread. More baklava. More crumbly cookies dusted with powdered sugar. And *Thee-ples*, her specialty of folded air bathed in honey. Then we were guided in our second stupor to open more presents, more new clothes under the tree. "Just what I always wanted," we'd been told to say when surprised by a new pair of socks.

Stuffed with two Christmas dinners and two second helpings, we sat and stared while the adults talked and visited for what seemed like hours. We were stunned stupid and wordless with the food of grandmotherly love until darkness came and we finally went home.

Christmas dinner without second helpings would have been a failure of love. For weeks before Christmas, my mother reminded us of how our old grandmothers would be working for days to prepare the stupendous meals. Not to eat everything on your plate meant you were an ungrateful child who didn't love his grandmother. So we ate until we couldn't move, returning the shared language of love our grandmothers understood.

Memories

Christmas in the Early 1900s

EDNA MICHAEL

For residents of the tiny village of Muncie in Vermilion County, Danville was the place to shop at Christmastime. But Christmas was an intimate community and family affair.

Just as the children of today look forward to the Christmas holidays, we, who were small children in the early 1900s, also dreamed about Christmas for many weeks before the wonderful day. We could look forward to being taken to Danville by our parents, once or twice during the month of December, to visit the two big department stores as well as the "dime store." This gave us an opportunity to see the toys and decide which ones we would put on our list. The trip was much more involved than it is today because our mode of transportation to the city was the Interurban Street Car, which ran between Springfield and Danville. The station was on South Vermilion, and I remember that the walk from there through the business district was very tiring for a child.

The most alluring toy for a little girl was a china-headed doll with long-lashed eyes that opened, beautiful curly hair, and a kid skin body. She didn't walk, talk, or take a bottle, but to us she was a prize. The toys that appealed most to the boys were

Facing page: Lincoln and Douglas dressed for Christmas in Washington Park, Ottawa, by James Ballowe

wagons, tricycles, trains, and bicycles. This was long before days of battery-run toys and ten-speed bicycles.

Besides looking at toys and getting money to shop by ourselves in the dime store for gifts for our parents, we sometimes got a pair of new shoes and material for some homemade clothes. The Christmas programs were an important social event for us, and we always wanted to be dressed up in our "Sunday best."

We practiced and presented little programs at school, but the big event was Christmas Eve at the church. We had two churches in Muncie—the Christian and the Baptist—but on Christmas Eve the members of each church took turns serving as host to a community celebration. Some of the men of the congregation would go to the woods to find and cut down an enormous pine tree that would almost reach to the ceiling of the church. The women would spend many hours decorating it with tinsel, strings of popcorn and cranberries, colored paper chains, and other homemade decorations. There was no electricity in the village, so there were no flashing lights or any other electrical devices, but we thought the tree was a work of art. Most of the families in the community did not have a Christmas tree in their homes, as we do today, so each family would bring one or two gifts for each child, to be placed on the church tree. Most of the little children really believed the gifts were from Santa Claus.

The first part of the evening was devoted to the Children's Christmas program. Many of us had difficulty remembering our little speeches because we were too occupied wondering which gifts we saw on the tree were the ones we had wanted. The big moment came when we would hear the sound of sleigh bells coming in our direction, and then Santa would enter with his bag of toys. He would have an orange (a rare treat in those days) and a bag of hard Christmas candy for each child. Then he would deliver all the presents on the tree. Some of the teenagers took advantage of the celebration to play tricks on each other, such as putting a beautifully wrapped gift on the tree for a friend, though the package contained something other than a gift.

After the community service, we returned to our homes to hang our stockings on the fireplace, place some food for Santa on the table, and hope he would visit us during the night. Somehow we always managed to awaken unusually early on Christmas morning, and we were never disappointed. We were always very satisfied to receive just a few gifts. (The days of TV advertising which entices children to want more and more toys were a long way in the future.)

The morning was always a very busy and exciting one for my brother and me, because it involved taking a seven-mile ride in the sleigh to our grandparents' home near Newtown, Illinois, for a family dinner. We had a beautiful sleigh, and our father may have used it other times during the winter, but I only remember the Christmas Day ride, because the horses always had sleigh bells attached to their harness. Much preparation had to be made before we could depart. Our team of Kentucky saddle horses had to be groomed, the sleigh had to be cleaned, bricks had to be heated and wrapped for foot warmers, heavy fur lap robes had to be warmed, some "goodies" for dinner had to be packed, and then we were on our way.

The relatives didn't get together very often during the year, so we really looked forward to seeing our cousins and enjoying a bountiful meal.

Grandmother always raised turkeys and geese, but turkey was our Christmas meat. White potatoes, sweet potatoes, squash, and cabbage were dug from underground storage; home-canned beans, peas, and tomatoes were our vegetables, and the relishes came out of big jars of spicy-smelling vinegar weighted down with a big clean rock. There was fruit cake, pumpkin, and mincemeat pie for dessert.

My mother usually took the pies that she had been busy preparing the previous day. We hadn't heard of canned pumpkin, so she made the pumpkin filling from scratch by baking the raw pumpkin in the oven for a long time and then scraping it out of the shell. The mincemeat filling was also made from raw materials. On butchering day, the tender meat on the calf's head was cooked for a long time and then shredded. To this mother added chopped apples, suet, raisins, currants, citron, sugar, fruit juices, and spices. I can still remember the fragrance that drifted through the whole house on the morning that she cooked the mixture. She always saved a small amount in the pan for my brother and me to taste when she canned the mincemeat. You can be certain that we were on hand for the treat.

Christmas afternoon, while most of the adults visited, we children would take time out of our playtime to gather around our grandfather's chair to listen to him recite poetry and tell interesting stories about the olden days. We had to listen carefully because he still retained some of the Scotch brogue from his forefathers.

The end of the day always came much too soon, but we didn't have headlights on the sleigh so we had to get home before dark.

Even though we lacked some of the modern conveniences in those early years, we did have something which I consider far more important for the survival of our democratic society—close community and family association.

Childhood Memories

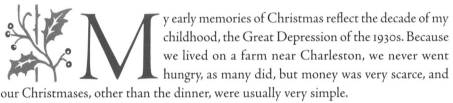

CAROLYN NEAL

The Great Depression of the 1930s defined the meaning of Christmas for many, as this story by a retired school teacher, now living in Kankakee, attests.

My early memories of Christmas reflect the decade of my childhood, the Great Depression of the 1930s. Because we lived on a farm near Charleston, we never went hungry, as many did, but money was very scarce, and our Christmases, other than the dinner, were usually very simple.

The first food preparation started with the making of our traditional dessert, English plum pudding. It was probably traditional because my mother's father was English, having come to the United States in the late 1870s. Mother always made plum pudding several weeks before Christmas. Plum pudding does not contain plums. It does contain raisins, currants, candied orange or lemon peel, citron and spices, plus the best freshly ground beef suet from the butcher shop. This was mixed with all the other ingredients and moistened with home-canned grape juice. Adding brandy would have been unheard of in our teetotaler household.

If she could afford it, Mother made enough to last all winter. She would pack it tightly in one-gallon milk crocks. She often used two crocks for our family of six. After the tops were covered with flour sacks and tightly tied down, the crocks were placed in water, where the pudding steamed for hours.

Most of the ingredients of our holiday dinner came from the farm itself. A typical Christmas dinner centered around a freshly caught, dressed, and baked hen served with dressing. If they could afford to buy oysters, it was oyster dressing. Mother always left one corner with oysters omitted just for me. The table was laden with mounds of mashed potatoes with gravy, candied sweet potatoes, green beans, scalloped corn, Waldorf salad, pickles, homemade rolls, and topped off with the English plum pudding. The pudding was sliced, heated in a granite pie pan in the oven of our coal range, and topped with hot vanilla or lemon sauce sprinkled with a dash of nutmeg.

Before her death when I was only six years old, my grandmother Watkins was often present. However, it was usually just the six of us—my parents, my brothers Edwin and Edgar, who were fifteen and eighteen years older than I, and my sister Alice, five years older than I.

Gifts were never numerous nor expensive, even in the better years. They were often handmade and simple. Most of the time I received needed clothing.

One year money was especially scarce. Although my parents had managed an orange, which was a special treat in those days, in my stocking hung on the mantel, the only thing I found under the tree that year was a small flat green purse, made of something not much sturdier than cardboard. It was in the outline of a Scottie dog and decorated with a small, flat metal medallion on the front.

I can still remember my disappointment that there was nothing more, and how I tried very hard not to show it, because I didn't want Mother and Daddy to feel bad. I had figured out where Santa's gifts came from, and heard my parents talking about not having money. They usually talked about such things after they thought I was asleep.

Oranges

VIRGINIA LONG

Oranges at Christmas were precious Christmas gifts for many Illinois citizens in the 1930s. This retired nurse, now living in Manteno, remembers how fate brought the pleasure of oranges to her family one Christmas.

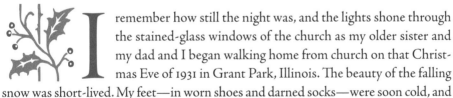I remember how still the night was, and the lights shone through the stained-glass windows of the church as my older sister and my dad and I began walking home from church on that Christmas Eve of 1931 in Grant Park, Illinois. The beauty of the falling snow was short-lived. My feet—in worn shoes and darned socks—were soon cold, and Daddy picked me up and put me up on his strong but stooped shoulders. He warmed my feet with his gloveless hands as I snuggled against his wool cap.

The walk home seemed endless, but I wanted it that way. I knew Santa Claus wasn't going to stop at our house. He had presents to bring to other houses, but we knew he wouldn't have anything for us. That's what we were told. We knew times were hard. We accepted the fact that this would be a holiday without toys . . . as well as any young child could.

Daddy lit the kerosene lamp when he returned home. In its light, I saw that we all looked like snowmen. My sister brushed us all off with a broom as he stood in a corner by the wood box. I was anxious to see the candles on our Christmas tree. We knew that they had served us for several years so they were pretty stubby. We knew that we couldn't let them burn very long.

I sat by the stove—in my own little rocking chair—to warm up. I could hear the crackle of corn cobs as Daddy stoked the fire. The contentment overtook me, and the next thing I knew everyone was saying, "Wake up ! Wake up! See what Santa brought!" I blinked my eyes sleepily but quickly jumped up when I saw the glowing candlelight on the tree.

And underneath it, a big box of plump oranges! Oranges that we could never buy at the store because we needed beans and flour. Oranges that I had only smelled and never remembered tasting! Santa did come!

Then on my way to bed, I saw the burlap bag hanging on the back door. It was the same sack that I had seen Daddy carrying many times with coal. He had carried it that day, in fact, when he was called to work. He worked for the railroad and there had been a derailment. He was called in to work on the tracks.

It didn't occur to me until later that there were rumors that this train was carrying fruit from the south. And did that gunny sack that Daddy carried . . . did it smell like oranges?

In my dreams that night—I still remember this—I saw Daddy with a long white beard and the burlap sack. And I saw him putting those oranges under the tree. So Santa Claus did come to our house. Even though he didn't have a Big Present, he did come.

Christmas Comes Early for Thatch

RON HORNBERGER

How fellow workers in Cairo came together at Christmas to rectify the misfortunes of a fellow citizen from the "suburb" of Future City is a story of giving often repeated throughout the state.

The one-story structure was not the type to be featured in *Better Homes and Gardens*, but the plastic sunflowers whirling in the wind and the pots full of other plastic flowers suggested joy and happiness. Alone inside lived a seventy-two-year-old man, whose wife had died almost six years ago. Also inside were his wife's piano, the family pictures, and other irreplaceable personal items. For Norvinia Thatch of Future City, Illinois, this was home.

But on December 13, while he was at work, his home was reduced to a smoldering shell as fire crept through the small padlocked rooms which hindered firemen from saving the home. Gone were his clothes, his cooking stove, his wife's piano, the family pictures—everything but the clothes on his back. "I lost everything but the best thing—my life," he would later comment.

His thoughts raced back to his childhood when he had seen days when he didn't know where he would be staying or where the next meal would be coming from, days when he had never seen his mother and had been raised by another woman. Being homeless wasn't going to make for a very Merry Christmas—or a Happy Birthday either, for his birthday fell on Christmas Eve. "I felt lost and down—the fourth time I been burned out," he said.

But the Farrow Lumber company, where he worked just north of Cairo, had some plans to lift his spirits. The company bought a used trailer, and company employees placed it where his house had burned down. His boss, Terry Farrow, told him that "we'll settle after Christmas." That sounded like a fair deal to Norvinia, who has worked at Farrow Lumber company and its predecessor since 1943. "It wouldn't be right for me not to pay for it," he observed.

But he still needed a place to stay until the trailer was finished. In the office of the company was a room where "breaks" could be taken, but it serves an additional duty now. When Norvinia gets off work at 3:30 P.M., he heads home—to the break room which the company has made available for him to use until the trailer is finished.

He had a place to stay, but what about food, clothes, and money? Some of his fellow employees chipped in with money to buy clothes, and other employees brought sandwiches with them to work and gave them to him.

Norvinia's outlook for Christmas, and the future, is a lot brighter now. "Brother, I got friends I never even thought I had," he said. "I'll be honest; people been so nice it brings tears to my eyes. They say after the trailer's set up, we'll have some more things too. I feel real uplifted; I really believe I'll be in the trailer by Christmas. I've had marvelous things done for me."

Maybe these marvelous things would have happened to Norvinia Thatch in the spring or the summer or the fall of the year. Maybe Christmas had nothing to do with it. But on the other hand, don't marvelous things happen at Christmas?

The Christmas Fox

EDGAR ALLEN IMHOFF

This story of family life during Christmas in 1934 near the Kincaid Hills west of Murphysboro reminds the reader that minor miracles were needed during the Dust Bowl and the Depression if the holiday were to have any semblance of festivity.

It had been a poor summer for Dad. A bad fall followed, and then a worse winter. There were simply no jobs to be had: no work on the hardroad, no hired-man jobs on farms, no work at the shoe factory. Years later, Dad recalled that business activity decayed in the fall of 1934 like the frostbitten grasshoppers and the brown leaves lining the creek beds. He said that it looked like everyone and everything was just going to give up and die.

December came to our shack on the woody hill and found us ill-prepared to survive, let alone be festive. Christmas approached and Dad seemed to become silent and touchy. Two days before Christmas, in a particularly blue mood, he pulled on his boots and wandered a half-mile or so through the woods, for no special reason, to the coal mine Uncle Ray and he had opened by drifting into the side of the hill. They had hauled in a few pieces of battered farm machinery to use in hoisting and moving coal, which now sat idle in the snow.

As Dad walked around the mine portal, stamping to keep his feet warm, he caught a glimpse of something foreign snared in the hoist. It looked like a big fur collar of a coat. He came closer and realized it must be a dead fox—a big and rare silver one, at that. (Years later, when an old man, he told me that at first he could hardly bring himself to touch it.) He held his breath as his eyes ran over the splendid pelt, the leg snared in a wire loop, the black frosty eyes staring at him.

The first we knew of it, Dad showed up at the shack, whistling and carrying a stiff dead animal. He thawed the fox by the wood stove and began to skin it out. We kids made a game out of running around holding our noses and complaining about the smell.

That very day he tacked the pelt on a board, tucked it under his coat sleeve, kissed Mom goodbye, and hiked off to town.

A few hours later, Dad returned from his twelve-mile trip—he had caught a ride home. He came into the shack and put a big sack on the floor. Grinning and laughing he began to pull out oranges, cans of pork and beans, graham crackers, and peanut butter. Then came the presents.

Agnes got a Shirley Temple doll, and Charley must've gotten something he liked but I wasn't paying attention because here came mine: a beautifully painted tin trolley car station, in which two windup cars ran around a little circuit. All night long I kept waking up in the dark shack and reaching out to feel it placed right beside our bed.

Dad never saw another silver fox, and I'll bet no one ever again traded that remarkable a pelt in Murphysboro. And after that winter, things began to get better.

The Cannon House at Christmas

FRED BUTLER

The Danville home of Joseph ("Uncle Joe") Cannon, the Republican speaker of the U.S. House of Representatives from 1903 to 1911, was razed in the 1940s to make way for a grocery store. It had stood for the author as a "shining light" during Depression-era Christmas celebrations.

Christmas time in Danville during the thirties was a gay and exciting place indeed, especially to the youthful home from school for the holidays or those of us who were waiting to greet them. The semiformal dances at the Wolford and Elk's ballrooms, sponsored by local sororities and fraternities, were held nearly every night except for Christmas Eve and were attended by everyone in town. Everyone, that is, who had not reached the advanced age of twenty-five or more.

The whole town seemed to be decorated in some form or other, but the shining light of all had to be Uncle Joe's house at 420 North Vermilion Street. Its size and regal splendor of white painted brick made it especially good to decorate with the red and greens of Christmas, and as a young florist, I was delighted to be asked by Mrs. Helen LeSeure (Uncle Joe's granddaughter) to do the job. It not only was a large order but also a challenging assignment.

The front of the house was decorated with handmade holly wreaths and with red satin bows placed at the bottom of the rings, and these were hung in every window, upstairs and down. The large front doors received English holly wreaths with huge red bows, and just outside the door and also inside the hall were giant balls of mistletoe just in case someone came who was not a "Kissin' Cousin" and needed an excuse to kiss. Two huge Christmas trees (the largest in tow) were in the north and south bay windows, and these were decorated with the finest decorations gathered through the years from all over the world. The grand piano had a large brass bowl filled with shiny and prickly English holly, as did the hall table and just about every other table in the house. The great dining room of the north parlor, with its massive twenty-foot table, was covered with imported linens, fine china and silverware, and beautiful candelabra. Red candles were used here, and the center of the table had three bowls of red carnations and English holly down its entire length.

The Cannon House at Christmas, ca. 1920s

Party night at the Cannon House was Christmas night, and that was an event that was truly something to behold. The guest list must have included nearly all the prominent families in Danville and vicinity and out-of-town friends of the family. The gracious hostess (Mrs. LeSeure) had seen to every detail, and it was most impressive to a "young man about town." The dining-room table was now filled to capacity with good food of all kinds, and colorful fruit and nuts too. Turkey, ham, and roast beef were served on large silver trays, and all the side dishes that made up a bountiful feast were on the "great table" for each guest to make his own selection. After a few glasses of champagne and food from this table of everything, we were off to dance at the Hotel Wolford feeling we had already had a great evening.

In recent years many a grocery cart has been pushed across the parking lot where this elegant house once stood, but the memory of Danville's number one citizen's home lingers on with many of us—especially at Christmas time.

Diary of a Farmer on Christmas, 1945

ANDREW DURDAN

A farmer near Grand Ridge records his family's daily preparations leading up to Christmas as the country was contemplating peace for the first time in four years.

(11 Dec. 45) I woke up this morning feeling light as a feather. With the corn harvest completed and the hard work of picking all of that corn behind me, I could now focus on the greatest time of the year—Christmas. This year seemed extra special. With Albert, Ray, and Michael home from the war, and Sully Kollar coming home for Christmas with his discharge right around the corner, it was going to be a Christmas to remember.

Before breakfast, I took Gladys to the Maple Grove School corner, then went to a sale with my brother John to a farm east of Ransom. We didn't buy anything, just enjoyed relaxing a bit and talking with the regular auction shoppers. After dropping John off at his place and visiting with Anna, I decided to make my way back to the school to pick Gladys up.

"What do you say we head over to Hallet's Nursery and pick up a Christmas tree?" I asked Gladys as she jumped into the car. "Your Uncle John mentioned they just got some fresh trees in."

"Why sure, but we better make sure that we get home in time for Mother to go to the club tonight," said Gladys. Mabel had a meeting with the Royal Neighbors club. They met during the holidays to make Christmas gifts for the needy. Tonight was the night to start the drive.

Gladys and I picked out a real pretty blue spruce from the nursery's fresh shipment and headed home.

The kids were home and were so excited to see the tree. Mabel had dinner ready and was a little antsy to get going.

I got the tree all set up in the stand and leveled it out.

"Can we decorate it tonight?" Esther asked, as she was eager to get started.

"Not tonight, Esther. We need to wait for Mom. We can do it tomorrow as soon as you get home from school."

(12 Dec. 45) Just before lunch I went up into the attic and found the Christmas boxes and hauled them down into the living room to get ready for decorating. I untangled the strings of lights and inspected for faulty bulbs.

After dinner Mabel, the three little ones, and Gladys decorated the tree. Mabel turned on Perry Como on the Philco. We had just finished putting up the lights when Darlene came home.

"How was your day?" Mabel asked Darlene.

"Very busy as usual," Darlene replied. "What can I do?"

"Well, we could use your height to put some ornaments near the top," I said, handing Darlene an ornament with her name on it. Mabel had made each of our girls an ornament, five different colors, with their names on the side with shiny glitter. After the lights and ornaments came the strands of paper rope and silver icicles. It was my job every year to put the angel on the top and then connect the power cord to light the tree.

"Oh, I need to set up the manger," Mabel said as she shuffled around looking for the manger in the boxes on the floor. "Andy, did you pull the box with the manger out of the attic?"

" Well, I guess not. Let me go have another look."

Mabel loved her manger with Mary, Joseph, and baby Jesus. She always set it up in the living room. The manger was good-sized and was made out of cardboard—and it was quite old.

I came back in just a few minutes with the manger boxes. Mabel was happy. She and Nancy set it up in the same place as the previous years.

"Mabel, I found something else in the attic that we need to put up," I said, hiding the mistletoe behind my back.

She smiled as I pulled the mistletoe from behind my back, raised it above her head, and gave her a kiss on the cheek and said "Merry Christmas." I then hung the mistletoe in the middle of the room.

Christmas had officially begun at the Durdan household.

(17 Dec. 45) Quite a lot of snow had fallen last night to add to the already treacherous conditions. Got Nancy, Esther, and Joyce all bundled up and ready for school. Today was the Christmas party for the parents. They had prepared for the better part of two weeks for this event.

At around 1:00 P.M., Mabel and I headed up the road to the school for the party. Everyone was starting to catch the holiday spirit. Miss Kates was buzzing around getting everyone in place for the holiday chorus. Mr. Todd, the school district's music director, was there on this special occasion. The kids sang Christmas carols—"Silent Night," "Hark the Herald Angels Sing," and "We Wish You a Merry Christmas." They also played a few numbers on their tonettes. Every once in a while one of the kids would miss a note on their tonette that would let out a shrieking sound. The parents chuckled. After the program, the kids presented their parents with the gifts hand-crafted in the schoolhouse. Then we enjoyed a variety of cookies that several mothers had volunteered to bring to the party.

(23 Dec. 45) Darlene spent the night at the Kollar's waiting for Sully to arrive. He had called three days ago to tell Darlene that he would hopefully be home by the twenty-second, but as of 10:00 P.M. last evening, he had not arrived. The phone rang at breakfast.

"He made it in, that's wonderful," Mabel replied to who I assumed was Darlene.

"What time did he get in?" I asked her.

"Two o'clock this morning," she replied. "He was stuck in Chicago for the past two nights. He came in on a bus."

"A bus? I thought he would come in on the train."

"Darlene said it was a real mess with thousands of soldiers and sailors trying to get home."

It started to snow just before lunch, and by the time Sully and Darlene arrived, the roads were covered with two inches of snow. We all ran outside to meet them. Sully looked great with a big smile, and Darlene looked so radiant. In fact, I don't believe I have ever seen her so happy.

Sully gave the little girls a big hug and said, "Let's go inside, girls. I bought each of you a present." The girls looked up at Sully with starry eyes. They had been talking about him all morning.

Inside, Mabel made coffee and served walnut cookies. The kids opened their presents from Sully—they each received a beautiful Christmas ornament. They were excited to hear that they were purchased in Chicago.

(24 Dec. 45) Sully was sleeping soundly on the couch this morning when I came out of the bedroom. Started the coffee and headed downstairs to stoke the coals and get the furnace going. Went outside and surveyed the roads a bit. The tire tracks from last night were all drifted over. I hustled back inside to see how to attack this morning's chores. Decided to get the Fordson going and plow the drive first, then tend to the animals.

Back inside, Mabel had quietly started putting breakfast together.

"It's blocked both north and south this morning. Don't think we'll be going anywhere anytime soon," I said.

"Good thing you got my oysters Saturday, and didn't wait until today," Mabel replied. She never missed a Christmas Eve without serving oyster stew.

"Does Sully like oysters?" I inquired.

"Sure he does. I asked him last night and he said that his mother makes oyster stew from time to time." She continued with a whisper, "but not as good as mine I'm sure." Mabel snickered.

We heard Sully stirring in the living room.

"Andy, go see if he wants some breakfast," Mabel prodded me to be a good host.

I stood up and met Sully halfway. He was tall, about my height, and slender. He had dark hair and had grown a mustache since the last time we saw him.

"Come join us for breakfast, Sully. We have fresh coffee, cereal, and toast," I said.

I got busy with feeding the animals and took a little extra time cleaning out the barn. I didn't mind spending more time in the barn, considering it was much warmer than being outside. Sully gave me a hand with shoveling around the entrances and around the new garage to clear the way if we were able to get out today.

We relaxed inside talking with Darlene, Gladys, and Sully through lunch. Sully wanted to see the 1939 Farmall F-30 that I bought this past May.

"Too early for a beer?" I asked Sully.

"Are you kidding me?" he replied. "Remember, you're talking to a navy man, Mr. Durdan." He laughed and followed me to the basement where I stored my Meister Brau. We walked out to the barn and looked at the tractor. We looked around a bit more and then headed back to the house.

Mabel's oyster stew was delicious. The only ones who didn't like the stew were Nancy, Esther, and Joyce.

"You'll like it one day, when you are older like us," I teased Nancy and Esther.

In addition to the oysters, I also purchased a quart of pickled pig's feet, which was my special Christmas Eve treat. One sight of those pig's feet and the girls ran for the hills.

(25 Dec. 45) As tradition prevails, we opened gifts on Christmas Eve. The little girls opened an array of gifts from us, along with some home-knitted hats, as Mabel was so practical. They opened fun things from Gladys and Darlene. The older girls gave me a nice new billfold, and Mom a bracelet. This morning the kids raced downstairs to see if Santa had been here and to see what he had put in their stockings the night before—oranges, Hershey bars, hard candy, and suckers.

(28 Dec. 45) We had flurries now and again throughout the week. Spent most of my time the past few days just doing my normal chores, tinkering around the machine shed and old garage, clearing the driveway and sidewalks of snow, and on occasion, pulling someone out of a ditch or helping someone get a car going. Sully and Darlene were spending precious time together before Sully had to return to the navy. They were starting to make plans for their wedding when Sully was discharged.

We normally kept the Christmas decorations through the new year, so the mood was still festive for the holidays. We were all getting a little bit of cabin fever.

(31 Dec. 45) We all went to Dad's for the New Year's Eve celebration this year. I believe everyone was there—all of my brothers and sisters, except for Mary and Milt. The house was full. Everyone seemed happy and content. This year certainly ended on a much higher note than it started. Albert and Ray were home, Sully was home and near coming home for good after his discharge, and Irene's husband Michael was home from the army. I thought of William Fraser who did not return, and all of those who gave their lives for our country so that we could live here in America in peace and freedom. We will start 1946 with a renewed sense of hope, starting our year without war. Gradually, our lives would return to normal.

At midnight, we raised our glasses to a new year. It wasn't until after 1:00 A.M. that the party died down. We found the three girls sleeping on their Grandpa's bed snuggled into the coats that were piled up there. Mabel picked up Joycie, and I woke up Nancy and Esther. We all got home and nestled into bed.

"Andy, could you please stoke the coals? It's quite chilly in here," Mabel asked.

"You betcha," I replied.

Holiday Memories

RUTH HANNA NOBLE

Ruth Hanna Noble, born in 1904, remembered this trip from Waukegan to Fairbury—nearly 150 miles—to her grandmother's farm on Christmas Eve, shortly before World War I.

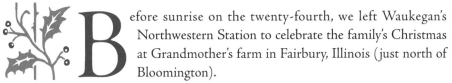

Before sunrise on the twenty-fourth, we left Waukegan's Northwestern Station to celebrate the family's Christmas at Grandmother's farm in Fairbury, Illinois (just north of Bloomington).

We changed first to the C&A Railroad, and then to the TP&W (locally called the "Tobacco, Pipes, and Whiskey"), which pulled us eastward from Chenoa into the dark night—a whole day's ride that is now a comfortable three-hour drive.

We spent the night with Uncle Harold, who roused us early Christmas morning for the final ride to Grandmother's house five miles away in a vast, snowy world reflecting brilliant sunshine. With horses prancing and sleigh bells ringing, his wagon pulled up from the barn. Runners replaced wheels, and we rode in the back, snug among big stones heated in the oven and carefully wrapped in woolen clothes. We were covered by an old buffalo robe, long ago sent back from the west by a mountain-man uncle. A deep layer of hay covered all this.

At Grandmother's, a swarm of uncles, aunts, and cousins laughed and reminisced, crowding the old house while waiting for Santa. At last a jingling of bells announced his arrival behind the closed doors to the parlor. For a moment, as the double doors opened, we forgot even Santa Claus because of the room's breathtaking beauty. The Christmas tree reached to the high ceiling, and on every branch and twig a lighted candle flamed.

Memories of the rest of the day are confused except for two things. One is the little automobile that ran all by itself after someone wound it. Minutes after receiving it, I found it broken with pieces neatly lined up by the curious cousin who, years later, satisfied that curiosity with bigger cars in Michigan.

Christmas in Naperville

MARIE ROSE ELLIS

With unerring detail, Marie Rose Ellis invites her readers to share her early-twentieth-century Illinois Christmas.

At the request of several nieces, I, Marie Rose Ellis (née Germann), will endeavor, with pleasure, to recall and note some incidents, events, and historical data regarding the Henry Adam and Anna Elizabeth (Stenger) Germann family. Some I recall, and some has been told to me by my parents or by my older brothers and sisters. I was the youngest of our family, born May 28, 1901.

Christmas was our big holiday. It really began on December 6, on St. Nicholas Day. We hung our stockings on the fireplace shelf the night before, then awakened

Marie Rose Ellis at the Germann Home, ca. 1920

the next morning to goodies never considered everyday fare, including oranges and candy. Oranges were not easily available in Illinois at that time.

On December 24 the large music room on the south side of the home was off-limits for the younger ones, because Santa's helpers were busy working. On this day, a large tree eight or ten feet high was delivered to the Stenger home, later the Germann home, by the Von Oven Nurseries in Naperville. The Von Ovens were friends of the Stengers for several generations, originally in Germany. It took some time to trim this large tree. We had probably twenty to twenty-five candles on it. Electric lights, a string of eight, were first used in 1920. While working in Chicago, my first job, I saw this new gadget displayed in one of Marshall Field's windows. It was December 1920, my first position, and I was having an adventurous time shopping.

Speaking of tree displays, in or about 1912, Henrietta came home to Illinois to visit, since Pauline had visited in Oregon and Henrietta came home with her so as to have help with Frank Jr. and Anna Marie. While shopping in Chicago with Minnie, Henrietta saw a new tree-base display at Marshall Field's. It was a musical base. She bought one for our home and one for her home in Astoria. The box base played several

Christmas carols. One thought comes to mind: before 1920 we always had the lighted candles only—no electricity—and running in and out of the music room, with the candles burning, we never had a tree catch fire. We were used to carrying candles to the cellar for supplies and were always cautioned to be careful. We used lamps entirely until 1915, when we had a gas line extended and then had a few gas lamps installed and a three-burner stove with iron legs set on a table in the kitchen. Carl engineered and talked Mother into this. Since we did not own the home, we never made radical changes, just papered and painted and replaced necessary items.

On December 24, we believers were kept in the kitchen with grandfather. He always entered into the Bavarian Christmas wholeheartedly. He had two rooms with a large closet opening to each room where we younger ones would play hide and seek, or we would sometimes fall asleep by the stove he had for heating. Soon we would hear the jingle bells! Dad swinging the length of bells used on the horse's harness during sleigh rides. Then we would hear a delicate horn blow (the angel's horn). That was the signal that Santa was arriving with bells and Kris Kindlein (Christ Child) with music. We were ready in the large music room around the tree. Santa rapped loudly on the front door and came in. "Has everyone been good this year?" Of course we were! He handed out gifts, spoke to us a few minutes, then left.

Then our mother spoke to us of the Christ Child. Santa meanwhile was hiding in the front hall—we thought he had left. Soon "Kris Kindelin" entered—the Christ Child spirit. A woman dressed in sheer white material and veiled. We never saw her face, she never spoke. We sang the Christmas carols for her, then knelt and prayed. This was to verify we knew our main prayers. All this time Grandfather was smiling in the background, leaning on his two canes.

Following Santa and Kris Kindlein's visits, we children were busy around the tree in the music room, opening and admiring our gifts. Besides those from Santa, we had some from Aunt Barbara Egermann, Aunt Julia and Uncle Theodore Ricksher, Aunt Mary Bapst and Aunts Mary and Emma from Aurora. Aunt Emma Stenger Germann was Louis's godmother, and he always received something extra from her. I was always interested in this gift because it was usually something both of us could enjoy—perhaps a rocking horse or a sled. I always got something special from our older cousin, Mrs. Ed Deiter (Josephine Egermann), because she was my godmother.

After the Santa years passed, we were always interested in the boxes arriving from Oregon—from Henrietta in 1909, Evelyn in 1916, from Magdalen in 1920, and from Minnie in 1921. This was during the years that Dad, Mother, Pauline, Louis, and I were still in the old home. To our last Christmas there, the tree, lights, and the old customs of services at church and our regular meal fare were observed the same. In the last ten or twelve years August and family, and also Carl and family, visited us. August always brought the children on Christmas Eve and again the next day for dinner, if Grandma Deiter did not have her invitation in before ours. Carl and Emma always came out from Chicago on Christmas Day. They came via railroad, and it meant a probable two-and-a-half-hour ride. They came out along with Anna and Al and returned the same evening.

On Christmas Eve, while we were enjoying our gifts around the tree, the older ones were helping Mother with the Christmas Eve supper. It was a day of fast, and the fare was always the same, oyster stew and crackers, scrambled eggs, cabbage salad, freshly baked coffee cake, and cookies. After supper the older ones and parents went to church for confessions. We younger ones, attending school, had gone in the afternoon when the others were glad to get rid of us for an hour or two in order to prepare for Santa and wrap gifts.

Early retirement was a rule for all. At 4:00 A.M. on Christmas we were up preparing to attend 5:00 A.M. mass at church. Usually we pushed through snow on foot the seven blocks and never thought of riding this distance as there were too many sleighs and cutters along the streets bordering the church and school grounds, with the horses blanketed well and tied to railings.

All of us in the school choir assembled in the belfry room, above the choir loft. There was an opening around the three or four large bells, and our voices carried outside as well as faintly inside the church proper. Then the large choir, or adult singers, in the choir loft below began the music and singing. I recall Theodore Boecker usually starting with "Holy Night" on his violin, then our cousin, Miss Lena Egermann, organist and director, led the choir in singing the mass and carols. A number of older men, once choir members, would join the choir in the loft along the side, until it seemed the rafters would split with vibrations. During this singing the children's choir from the belfry was coming down the two flights of wood stairways, passing the adult choir and on to the main church floor. As soon as we arrived, a signal was given by the nuns ordering us quietly to seats in the front, left side, just a few feet from the large crib display. While the organist played "Ihr Kinderlein kommet" (Come ye little children), we sang it at the crib. A high mass in Latin followed with the adult choir singing in Latin. They sang many carols during mass and later as people departed. Following the service, everyone greeted friends shuffling in the snow on the sidewalks, or at the sleighs and cutters with teams tied to the rails.

After greeting friends, we walked home. By this hour, the bells in all the churches were summoning members for services. I recall that all of them had different tones to their bells, as some were single and small and much in contrast to our large bells. There were tones from Episcopal, Lutheran, Methodist, Brethren (Holy Jumpers), Congregational, and Evangelical, and everyone greeted each other in passing by.

After fasting from midnight, we were ready for that great midwestern breakfast. Mother was always at the lead with our older girls, heading home to get things going. There would be home-canned fruit, pork sausage, potatoes, all from the well-stocked cellar, and also fresh-baked Kuchen (coffee cake) and frosted Christmas cookies, along with many of Mother's special cookies and breads from family recipes—Zimmt Stern (stars), Mandelbrod (almond cookies), Mandelschnitz (almond cuts), and many others. Mandelbrod was really more like modern-day brownies in that it was dark brown and not a cookie. Many of the old recipes had spices in them which changed the color of the finished product. Milk and coffee were also served.

This was always a joyful time for all of us, for seldom did we all assemble for breakfast at one time or serving.

Following our breakfast, Evelyn and Magdalen did the dishes, Marie carried them to the cupboards, the older ones helped Mother prepare the Christmas dinner and also straightened up the music room and front parlor, always disarrayed from Christmas Eve. Our fare for Christmas dinner was usually a goose and the trimmings or sometimes several ducks, if the geese had not been hatched the spring before.

Christmas Comes

SARAH BUNTING

Sarah Bunting began her teaching career in 1922 at Green School, a one-room school three and a half miles east of Alvin, Illinois. What happened the following Christmas made her decide on teaching as a career.

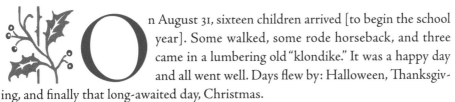 n August 31, sixteen children arrived [to begin the school year]. Some walked, some rode horseback, and three came in a lumbering old "klondike." It was a happy day and all went well. Days flew by: Halloween, Thanksgiving, and finally that long-awaited day, Christmas.

Minnie, an eighth-grade girl, and I made new curtains for the windows. The two boys of grade eight secured the top of an old apple tree to the stage and, undaunted by the fact we could not buy a Christmas tree, wrapped this tree in cotton. The first four graders made large Santa heads with snowy white cotton whiskers. Large deer heads were made and colored, and Santa and Rudolph were hung amidst festoons of colored-paper chains. Gifts had been made for mother and father and wrapped in white tissue, secured by a beautiful gummed Christmas sticker. Standing shining and polished was an old pump organ bought for this special occasion with the eight dollars gleaned from a box-supper in October. Every song and recitation had been learned to perfection, and all was ready for our Christmas-night spectacular. The tree, we agreed, was lovely with store tinsel, colored candles, and decorations made by the children. When it was dark, we banked the fire, locked the door, and went home happy in the thought of how beautiful it all was.

At 7:00 the next morning we arrived, starry-eyed, with spirits high, knowing examinations would be over by noon and the lovely dreams we had dreamed would become realities.

Opening the door, we were shocked by what greeted us. A cloud of black smoke and soot engulfed us. The stove had blown up, and festoons of soot hanging from the branches of our beautiful white cotton tree had ruined it. Each smiling Santa Claus face was graced by dirty black whiskers, and every reindeer wore a harness of soot. The lamp chimneys were smoked, and it was impossible to see through the dirty windows! And our new curtains! Need I describe them?

Standing in the doorway, we were dazed for a few minutes. There was a flood of tears from the little ones and only an occasional gulp from the older ones. Slowly we entered and began opening windows so we might more clearly determine the extent of the damage. The first- and second-grade pupils sat staring at me as though I had somehow purposely allowed their world to crash in upon them.

After a few moments of silence, I suggested the boys carry in water from the old, creaking pump. This we put on to heat. I drained some kerosene from the range tank, and we washed the seats and desks. Then, reminding the children there was work to be done, we sang "Good Morning to You" and "America." By this time an almost happy atmosphere had developed, so we began writing the county superintendent's final examinations.

Noon came, exams were over, and everyone settled quietly for lunch. After lunch, Minnie, grade eight, rode her horse home, laundered the curtains, and returned in about two hours. Grades four, five, and six recovered the Christmas tree with cotton. Eighth-grade boys gave Santa heads some clean white whiskers and freed Rudolph's antlers from the strings of soot. First-, second-, and third-grade pupils washed dishes, pans, and even lamp chimneys.

Then behold, the final catastrophe! Teacher climbed the ladder, stretched high, pulled hard, and out came the flue-stop. Poof! Down the ladder came a very sooty, dirty teacher. Everyone had a good laugh, and though it meant more scrubbing and cleaning, everybody worked with a will.

At 4:00 P.M. we went home. Arriving back at 7:00, shining and very happy, we started our program at 7:30. At 9:00, as the last persons filed out of the school, these words rang in my ears: "It was the nicest Christmas program ever held here."

That night, as I mentally reviewed the happening of the day, I knew I wanted to be a teacher. My childhood dreams had come true. I was sure there would never be a circumstance I could not overcome so long as I could be surrounded by the trust and devotion of children.

Many other things happened in that year and the next that I spent in that school. Some were good, some bad, some tragic, but mostly happy. Born into my being that night was the resolution to devote my life to children, and I did. There were hard times, small pay, many inconveniences, but these were the "fires that tempered the steel" of my teaching career which ended forty-five Christmases later in 1967.

Christmas Eve in the Barn

JIM MAY

The author, a prize-winning storyteller, lives on a small farm on Nippersink Creek, which runs through McHenry and Lake Counties. Here he reminds his audience that an essential meaning of the Christmas story is that the chance to provide sanctuary and kindness to the poor and homeless is a blessing.

When I was a boy in the fifties, on Christmas Eve I would be sent to the barn to help my dad milk cows. I'd be forced to leave the warmth and cheer of that old farm house for the pungent chill of the barn where the only warmth was the steam rising from the huge bodies of our friendly milking Holsteins. I wasn't much help milking for I'd spend the night standing sentry next to the heavy, wooden, double doors at one end of our dairy barn, watching for Santa Claus, while the sweet scent of bovine, silage, and manure rose past me and out into the night through the crack I had made between the doors. I knew he and the reindeer were out there because there were always presents under the tree when Dad and I returned from chores.

On one particular Christmas Eve, while I stood at my usual station—alert for the appearance of the magical elf—a dull thump from above startled my dad and me. We climbed the ladder into the hayloft to investigate and found an old man warming his hands over a candle, the clear flame perfectly still in the cold air. I had seen hobos riding the train and sometimes walking the tracks. I always imagined that they were going to Chicago or maybe out west. He explained that he'd been out looking for work, but that it was scarce, and now he was on his way home. The train he'd been riding had pulled up on the sidetrack over in the farm supplies yard. "I couldn't sleep there, too cold. I saw the barn and figured the cows here would keep it warmer than the boxcar."

His face was scarred and dirty and bruised purple—like the faces of other hobos I had seen. Dad said it was the dust and cinders working into the skin of these men who rode the rails. He had a blanket wrapped around him, but he looked cold. He was bare-headed and his hair was thin but long, down below his collar.

Dad said he was sorry but that he had no work to offer. The old man said he'd only stay the night. "I just wanted to get a little warm here tonight, then I'll be goin', gotta get home by Christmas Day or my family'll be worried. I got a boy just about your little fella's age. Yeah, I gotta get to Chicago Christmas Day. Train will be through here in the morning."

Dad asked him if he wanted to come into the house to eat and to warm up. He said he'd be all right in the barn until morning.

While Dad and I looked on he began his eating routine. Perhaps embarrassed by his situation, he wanted to show us he could get along—that he had food and a plan. We watched him lift a tin can out of a burlap sack. Eyes fixed intently, his thick, cracked fingers worked a small pocketknife blade in a tight, jagged circle, steadily, patiently, like he was familiar with the difficulty of this simple task. His face seemed older than Santa's had at the dime store, and his bruised skin shone through his stubby white whiskers. In fact his whole face glistened. Then I saw it in his lap—an empty jar of Vaseline jelly. I was glad he had put something on that sore face.

Dad and I walked back to the house. The snow bore witness to our excursion with tracks and squeaks as our shadows followed, caught up, and then passed us under the spray of the yellow yard light. I wondered how Santa could find one little family in a big city.

"Do you think Santa will bring the old man a present?"

"No, I think Santa mostly takes care of children," Dad answered.

"So his little boy will get a present?"

"I suppose he'll get something," replied Dad.

Inside our house Christmas had erupted everywhere. The tree was lit up and there were some toys and packages underneath. I ran into the living room, dropped to my knees, and slid across the floor. By the time I stopped I was under the Christmas tree. I looked up and there it was, just about at eye level, the plaid, bright, red and black felt hunting cap that looked just like the ones the hunters wore in my older brother's collection of adventure books. My best present was a plastic model horse, a golden brown and white pinto, its neck arched and its right leg raised in a high prance.

My parents, sisters, brother, and I sat close to each other, grateful for the tree and the presents and for what seemed the impossible beauty that had descended upon that cozy wallpapered living room.

After supper everyone got ready for Midnight Mass, except my father, who said he was getting too old to stay up that late and then milk the cows in the morning.

Before we left for church my mother asked me to take some food to the tramp in the hayloft. She made up a shoebox containing leftover smoked fish, dinner rolls, and a cloth napkin.

The church bells were ringing by the time we walked up the steps and into the vestibule of St. Peter's. It was nearly midnight but the whole town seemed alive, the sidewalks full of people.

Red ribbons adorned each of the pews, and there were tall Christmas trees in the sanctuary at the front of the church. We sat in the front of the church because the people who had come early got the seats in the back and in the middle.

The figurines of the Baby Jesus, Mary, Joseph, and the angels all seemed to have divine, beatific facial expressions. Even the cows and donkeys looked like saints, which made me think that animals must go to heaven. The church was full of good smells from the fir trees and incense.

Father's sermon was about how God had chosen a humble manger among animals for His Son's birthplace. I thought about the stranger in the haymow. While others were celebrating Christmas in their houses, in churches, and at parties, he was the one that was in a barn, just like the Christ child.

Then Father talked about the story of the Good Samaritan who helped a stranger who had been beaten and robbed and left to die by the side of the road. The Samaritan bound up the stranger's wounds and took him to a place of lodging where he could recover.

I thought about the tramp in our barn, and I hoped he would be home this Christmas Day so that someone could take care of him.

When we got home, my dad was still awake. He said the tramp had kept him up. Noticing the lights on in the milking barn, Dad had walked to the barn to find the hobo pacing up and down the aisle, talking about how he was going to own cows someday when he got back to his family. Dad said it took a while to coax him back up into the hayloft. He couldn't figure whether the tramp was dreaming or sleepwalking or if he had a bottle of whiskey or wine stashed somewhere. Dad said that the only thing he could smell on the man was smoked fish.

My father made some warm milk and some onion sandwiches, his favorite late-night snack. Everyone else went to bed, but I stayed up and told him about the Good Samaritan story. Dad said it was a good story and that farm people took a story like that to heart and that I should always remember it, but that I should also be careful around strangers and should never get into a car with one or anything like that. I said that I wouldn't.

Then I asked dad to tell me about his father, my Grandpa Pete, taking the whole family to church in the bobsled. Dad said that on the ride home you'd hear nothing but the muffled sound of the horses' hooves and once in a while a distinct sleigh bell from someone else riding home on the latest church night of the year.

Before I was down to the bottom of my cup of warm milk I asked dad again about the tramp's little boy and if he would get anything for Christmas. My dad said he wasn't sure what Santa would do but that he was sure Santa would do his best.

Then I must have fallen asleep because the next thing I knew Dad was bending over my bed and kissing me good night.

I woke up early on Christmas morning. I got dressed in a hurry and went straight for the hand cream on my mother's dresser. My dad had bought it for her on Mother's Day instead of the usual red geraniums. I had seen the cream in the Raleigh man's box of wares when he made one of his regular stops. The cream was called Lilacs in Paris. My mother, who was particular about such things, said it smelled more like a plain old American dog had lifted its leg on the lilacs, and she tried to throw it out. I convinced her to keep it for my father's sake, but we went back to geraniums on Mother's Day after that.

I thought the cream smelled all right, and even Mom said it felt soothing on her skin. I carried the hand cream into the living room, and grabbed the box with the toy horse from under the tree, and put the lavender jar into it.

I put on my old hat, stuffed the box under my coat, and dashed to the barn. I took my time climbing the hayloft ladder.

It was quiet in the hayloft and the candle had gone out. At first I thought I was too late, that he had caught his train. Then I heard snoring. I found him asleep, his rumpled blanket slowly rising and falling in time to his raspy, irregular breaths. His bare and balding head stuck out of the mound of covers like some weather-beaten turtle's.

I wondered if his father used to put him to bed, too. I wondered what dreams or hopes his father might have had for him. I didn't want to wake him up, so I left the box and climbed back down the ladder.

Inside, the smell of turkey was oozing out of the walls and furniture and I got myself a hot bath. Christmas Day was fun with all the cousins around. After dinnner we made a snow fort, and we stuffed ourselves with leftovers at suppertime. I fell asleep on the floor. That night, when Dad put me to bed, he said that he had seen the tramp get on a train about ten o'clock that morning.

I slept late the morning after Christmas. By the time I woke up, Dad had already milked the cows. He and Mom were at the table when I walked into the kitchen. It was cloudy outside and looked to me like the Christmas season had ended with a sudden gray thud.

My parents invited me to sit down at the table. My mother was smiling just a little, my dad a little more.

"I saw one of the train brakemen this morning," my dad said. "He gave me this for you." Dad reached alongside his chair and held up a brown paper bag. I couldn't understand what a railroad man would be giving me, especially with Christmas over. I looked in the bag. It was my pinto horse. I was happy to have it back, but then I thought about the tramp's son. I looked up at Dad.

"The brakeman said he saw the tramp jump a train heading north to St. Paul. He said the old fella's a regular, doesn't have a family or permanent address."

I looked down at the horse.

"Said he'd never seen the tramp so happy before, though, unusually tickled for a man alone on Christmas Day." Dad rattled the brown bag a little with his hand so that I looked back up at him.

"The brakeman said that some of the other hobos were teasing him about how good he smelled, like he had been soaking all night in lilac water. And he had the warmest headgear on the train, a new, red cap with warm, felt earflaps."

I looked back down. My face felt hot. My parents and I knew how much I needed that warm hat for the winter; my mom worked extra hours at the typewriter factory so that we could have nice clothes.

"I figured those things were mine," I said weakly.

"It's okay," said my mom. "I guess I'll just have to get used to having a Good Samaritan around the house."

I figured that the Good Samaritan had done me a good turn, too, since I had my horse back and hadn't gotten in trouble. After breakfast I picked up the bag and ran back into my room to play with the horse. I sat down on my bed and shook the pinto out of the bag. A jagged piece of shoebox fell out. It smelled like smoked fish. The heavy black marks printed on the cardboard looked as though they had been made by a wide, soft pencil. I took the cardboard into the kitchen to show my parents. My mother read the words to me, and then she put the note away in her closet with her prayerbooks and candles.

At Christmastime in later years, I would take the note out and read the words to myself:

Fer Gimmy the kid in the whit barn tanks for the cap is the bess one I iver haf in a lon time the crem feels soo goot kep da hors.

My Grandfather's Treasure

MARY MIRITELLO

Mary Miritello's late mother tells her the meaning of the presepio, *an elaborate handmade Nativity scene traditional in Italian-American households.*

For where your treasure is, there your heart will be also.
—Matthew 6:21

"We never had a Christmas tree when I was growing up," my mother explains. "My brothers and sisters and I wished we could be like everyone else on the block." Growing up in the 1920s on the South Side of Chicago, she looked with longing at the neighbors' windows, where green branches sparkled with tinsel and colorful ornaments. As the only Italian family on the block, the eight Fratto children knew that their Christmas traditions were unlike those of the Irish families who lived next door.

In this Armour Square neighborhood, successive waves of working-class ethnic groups had settled; first the Germans, then the Swedes, and by the last quarter of the nineteenth century, the Irish predominated. During the first two decades of the twentieth century, Italians began to settle in Armour Square and its adjacent neighborhood of Bridgeport. Looking for better housing, many Italians who had originally settled near the train station at Dearborn and Polk Streets in the Loop gradually moved south of the city's center as they sought to improve their living conditions. And so it was that my maternal grandfather, Saverio Salvatore Fratto, settled with his young family on a street within walking distance of Comiskey Park, the new stadium where the White Sox had just begun playing baseball in 1910. He was one of four million Italians who came to America between 1880 and 1920, and he was one of many thousands who settled in Chicago at the turn of the century.

A passerby walking on this street on a cold December morning in 1925 might have wondered whether the Fratto family had any holiday spirit whatsoever. But if the passerby were to knock on that heavy oak door and step inside, a grand display would tell, in a glance, that the true spirit of Christmas was vibrantly alive in this home.

*Saverio
Salvatore
Fratto's
presepio
Nativity
scene, 1945*

"Every year, in early December, we would remove most of the furniture from our living room in preparation for the *presepio*," my mother remembers. "Pa would set up a long table along the north wall, next to the fireplace." There he would begin assembling, little by little, the scenes and the figures that would tell the story of the birth of the Christ Child.

My mother remembers how cardboard boxes of different sizes would be positioned on the table to create the illusion of a hillside terrain. Then my grandfather would drape these boxes with sheets, preparing a base for the display. Working slowly, he would create vignettes of humble figures farming in their fields, carrying their bundles of wares to market, tending to their livestock, all going about their everyday lives. But amidst these scenes of chores and hard labor, there was something magnificent taking place. In the very center, at the bottom of the many-tiered display, was the Christ Child, with Mary and Joseph. "It seemed that all the roads were leading down to the manger," my mother explains. On these paths were many figures, all journeying toward baby Jesus. "My father would set each figure out with such care. He would add a statue, step back, studying the scene for a long time, as if he were trying to select just the right spot. He had so much patience."

No matter the time of year, the *presepio* was always on his mind. On walks during the spring and summer, my grandfather would stop to pick up twigs, rocks of interesting colors and shapes, bits of tree bark and small branches, empty cardboard matchboxes, and even the silver paper folded inside of discarded cigarette packs. Each found object could potentially add some new touch to the display. He took great pride in building the shepherds' huts, the farmers' houses, little structures made of wood and papier-mâché. "All summer long, in his spare time, Pa would be down in the basement, making something new," my mother recalls.

Throughout the Christmas season, their home was filled with friends and relatives who came to view the *presepio* and to pay homage to the newborn King. "My father would point out the new items and would answer questions about what he had tried to evoke in different scenes. I can still see him in my mind's eye, pointing out new items and answering questions."

After the Feast of the Epiphany on January 6, my grandfather would disassemble the tableau, taking his time to pack up each statue and each hand-built structure with loving care. In January 1936, he was even slower than usual in completing this task. He was quiet and not feeling himself. Then, on January 16, he suffered a sudden and fatal heart attack. My mother remembers that for many weeks thereafter, no one in the family could bring themselves to touch the boxes in the basement or to attempt to put them away on the shelves where they belonged.

When Christmas arrived in 1936, mourning still hung heavy on everyone's heart. In the years that followed, no one felt like celebrating the holiday. Soon, World War II loomed on the horizon, and sons Sam and Tony would leave home for military service. Now, a passerby would see a Christmas tree in the living room, with a star hanging in the window, showing that a family member was gone, serving his country. My mother cherishes a black-and-white photograph from 1945, capturing the family's Christmas tree, under which are nestled some of the original statues from my grandfather's *presepio*. Baby Jesus is still held in a manger fashioned from twigs, built by my grandfather's hand. The scene is simple, and two hand-built structures from the original *presepio* are positioned on the left and right. The twig-fashioned manger and the two buildings, captured in this photo, are the only glimpse I will ever have of what my grandfather constructed with his own hands.

At last, my mother finally had the Christmas tree she had always wished for as a child. At last, she realized that the *presepio* had been the family's great treasure, brought to life by the love and faith in her father's heart.

Mother and Daughter, Christmas Eve

CHANNY LYONS

From the Hudson River to Winnetka to Peoria, lighting candles on
Christmas Eve at dusk has been a ritual of recollection for the author.

Even as a very young girl I felt the solemnity of the silence—
and the feeling of warmth around my heart. I recognized
it then as I do now in the twilight of Christmas Eve and
the flickering candlelight reflected on the windowpanes. It
was our time—my mother's and mine—to nourish our attachment to each other . . .
to reflect on the infinite. It was a joyousness that calmed the spirit and contained my
natural instinct to dance, to twirl around the living room in front of the tree decorated
with beautiful ornaments.

We lived on a bluff along the Hudson River, west of New York City. The late afternoon light faded slowly into darkness as my mother and I lit the tall tapers and
placed them on the windowsills in the living room and dining room. It was our tradition. Earlier in the day Mom had affixed each candle to a small tin tray with a handle
and rolled edges to catch the dripping wax. To light the candles, she used long wooden
matches from an octagonal red and green box. Softly, on the record player Bing Crosby
sang carols and the Firestone Orchestra played more holiday music. Buttenheim, our
black-and-white Lab, curved his narrow body toward us in the provocative way he
had of letting us know he was with us. His tail wagged gently and he smiled.

We kneeled on the sofa that stretched under the living-room windows and watched
as the Messuris' lights came on across the street, and the Johnsons' in the house beyond theirs. The candlelight twinkled. Wax slid down the side of the candle, landing
on the tray. Mom held my hand, and I felt her goodness move from her hand to mine.
She was a magical woman, able to create scenes as a good writer does—and then wrap
you into them. She made it easy to recall the atmosphere of Christmas Eve.

Soon my Dad's car would turn onto Rose Hill Avenue and up our steep driveway
into the garage. Then a light supper and an early bedtime for me. For Mom and Dad,
there were more presents to wrap, maybe a ballerina tutu to finish sewing and hang
from the fireplace mantel.

Over the years we gazed out other windows at dusk. First, our family home in Winnetka north of Chicago, which had a series of French doors across the front of the house whose windows lacked sills. Mom innovated. She lined up candles along the edges of the tables at either end of the sofa and on the long dining-room table where their sparkling flames reflected in the windows and the mirror on the opposite wall. We lit the candles, the rooms softened, the silence enveloped us once again. We sat on the sofa or in the dining room, talked gently, held hands, and waited for Dad to pull in the driveway.

Mom's been gone for well over a decade now. My husband and I live in Peoria, and I wouldn't miss my chance to put a candle near the window in what Mom named my "terrace room," where the glass goes from the ceiling to the floor. When we first moved here thirty years ago, my dad hung Christmas lights on the hemlock tree in the far corner of the backyard. The tree looked brilliant, especially from the terrace room. Lighting trees was one of Dad's specialties. Over time the tree outgrew the lights and we took them down.

On Christmas Eve I light a candle using long wooden matches from an octagonal holiday box, and I watch the dusk settle into the woodland beyond the backyard. I talk to my mom, I remind her, and I feel her hand around mine. For a few minutes the world is in perfect balance once again.

Christmas at Thatchcot

VIOLET TROVILLION AND HAL W. TROVILLION

During the first half of the twentieth century, the cottage home of the Trovillions in Herrin was the location of one of the finer, and some say the oldest, private printing presses in Illinois. One of the ongoing productions of the press was a literary Christmas greeting by way of a small volume for which fortunate recipients waited eagerly each year. Here is an excerpt from one of the last of these booklets, in 1947.

Christmas to us has ever been a season filled with joyous excitement. It is the one day in the long calendar of the year in which we all seem to soften up and view the world as a friendly place to dwell. Most of the people about us appear to be friends and we deal with one another as if brothers in the flesh.

President Coolidge once attempted to define Christmas in these words:

> Christmas is not a time nor a season, but a state of mind. To cherish peace and goodwill, to be plenteous in mercy, is to have the real spirit of Christmas. If we think of these things, there will be born in us a Savior and over us will shine a star sending its gleam of hope to the world.

For a number of years now we have practiced the happy custom of greeting our friends at Christmas with a little book, a folder or a card printed on our private press. These little messengers of happy tidings have conveyed the Christmas spirit to homes of many friends here and abroad. They have made us known to those we knew not, and have brought the distant near and made a brother of the stranger.

One of the earliest Christmas books was *Thoughts from Robert Louis Stevenson*. It appeared in 1908, compiled by us from the writings of our favorite novelist. Three years later we brought out *Success and Failure*, a sermon from the famous Greek scholar, Benjamin Jowet, master of Balliol College, Oxford. A little while ago a second edition was printed on Tuscany handmade paper with an introduction written by Dr. William Lowe Bryan, president emeritus of the University of Indiana. Back in 1910 we published a volume from our own pen, *Neapolitan Vignettes*, an account of a trip to Italy. For our next book, we again turned to Stevenson. We compiled some of our favorite selections, including many of the prayers, and gave them the title of *Amphora of*

R. L. S. Love Letters of Henry VIII to Anne Boleyn was our next Christmas book. This volume was followed at intervals of one to three years with the following in the order here listed: *The Happy Prince, Francine's Muff, Vagaries from Munthe, Tussie Mussie, Favorite Fragments, The Selfish Giant, Another Tussie Mussie, In Casa Mia, The Sundial in Our Garden, The Private Press as a Diversion, In Country Places, First Garden Book, Delights for Ladies, Kipling Speaks to the Young Man, Old English Yuletide,* and *Christmas in Review.*

From time to time numerous cards, folders, and tracts were printed to carry Christmas messages to friends. As we look over some of these publications, they are filled with inspiring thoughts.

This is the end of
Christmas at Thatchcot

Of which seven hundred and eleven copies were printed on Van Gelder paper, in Baskerville type, for Violet and Hall W. Trovillion by Trovillion Private Press at the sign of the silver horse, Herrin, Illinois, in the fall of nineteen hundred and forty seven.

Mary and Joe Chicago-Style

MIKE ROYKO

This modern-day retelling of the Christmas story, related in the inimitable style of Mike Royko, has become a classic.

Mary and Joe were flat broke when they got off the bus in Chicago. They didn't know anybody and she was expecting a baby.

They went to a cheap hotel. But the clerk jerked his thumb at the door when they couldn't show a day's rent in advance.

They walked the streets until they saw a police station. The desk sergeant said they couldn't sleep in a cell, but he told them how to get to the Cook County Department of Public Aid.

A man there said they couldn't get regular assistance because they hadn't been Illinois residents long enough. But he gave them the address of the emergency welfare office on the West Side.

It was a two-mile walk up Madison Street to 19 South Damen. Someone gave them a card with a number on it and they sat down on a bench, stared at the peeling green paint and waited for their number to be called.

Two hours later, a caseworker motioned them forward, took out blank forms, and asked questions: Any relatives? Any means of getting money? Any assets?

Joe said he owned a donkey. The caseworker told him not to get smart or he'd be thrown out. Joe said he was sorry.

The caseworker finished the forms and they were entitled to emergency CTA bus fare to Cook County Hospital because of Mary's condition. And he told Joe to go to an Urban Progress Center for occupational guidance.

Joe thanked him and they took a bus to the hospital. A guard told them to wait on a bench. They waited two hours, then Mary got pains and they took her away. Someone told Joe to come back tomorrow.

He went outside and asked a stranger on the street for directions to an Urban Progress Center. The stranger hit Joe on the head and took his overcoat. Joe was still lying there when a paddy wagon came along and pinched him for being a drunk on the street.

Mary had a baby boy during the night. She didn't know it, but three foreign-looking men in strange, colorful robes came to the hospital asking about her and the baby. A guard took them for hippies and called the police. They found odd spices on the men, so the narcotics detail took them downtown for further questioning.

The next day Mary awoke in a crowded ward. She asked for Joe. Instead, a representative of the Planned Parenthood Committee came by to give her a lecture on birth control.

Next, a social worker came for her case history. She asked Mary who the father was. Mary answered and the social worker ran for the nurse. The nurse questioned her and Mary answered. The nurse stared at her and ran for the doctor. The doctor wrote "Post partum depression" on her chart.

An ambulance took Mary to the Cook County Mental Health Clinic the next morning. A psychiatrist asked her questions and pursed his lips at the answers.

A hearing was held and a magistrate committed her to Chicago State Mental Hospital on Irving Park Road.

Joe got out of the county jail a couple of days later and went to the county hospital for Mary. They told him she was at Chicago State and the baby had been placed in a foster home by the Illinois Department of Children and Family Services.

When Joe got to Chicago State, a doctor told him what Mary had said about the baby's birth. Joe said Mary was telling the truth. They put Joe in a ward at the other end of the hospital.

Meanwhile, the three strangely dressed foreign-looking men were released after the narcotics detail could find no laws prohibiting the possession of myrrh and frankincense. They returned to the hospital and were taken for civil rights demonstrators. They were held in the county jail on one hundred thousand dollars bond.

By luck, Joe and Mary met on the hospital grounds. They decided to tell doctors what they wanted to hear and were released.

When they applied for custody of Mary's baby, however, they were told it was necessary for them first to establish a proper residence, earn proper income, and create a suitable environment. They applied at the Urban Progress Center for training under the Manpower Development Program. Joe said he was good at working with wood. He was assigned to a computer data processing class. Mary said she'd gladly do domestic work. She was assigned to a course in key-punch operating. Both got twenty-dollar-a-week stipends.

Several months later they finished the training. Joe got a job at a gas station and Mary went to work as a waitress.

They saved their money and hired a lawyer. Another custody hearing was held, and several days later the baby was ordered returned to them.

Reunited finally, they got back to their two-room flat and met the landlord on the steps. He told them Urban Renewal had ordered the building torn down. The City Relocation Bureau would get them another place.

They packed, dressed the baby, and hurried to the Greyhound Bus station.

Joe asked the ticket man when the next bus was leaving.

"Where to?" the ticket man said.

"Anywhere," Joe said, "as long as it is right now."

He gave Joe three tickets and in five minutes they were on a bus heading for Southern Illinois—the area known as "Little Egypt."

Just as the bus pulled out, the three strangely dressed men ran into the station. But they were too late. It was gone.

So they started hiking down U.S. 66. But at last report they were pinched on suspicion of being foreigners in illegal possession of gold.

MEMORIES +

That Is Christmas

RICHARD KLEMP

Richard Klemp, now retired and living in Seneca, was a seven-year-old living in Forest Park when he delivered papers on his Christmas bike in River Forest in 1945.

Snow makes you think of Christmas when you are seven. Ever hide in the wooden bathroom in the basement, and hear Santa Claus come down the stairs? Of course, ten years later realizing it was Uncle Frank? Doesn't make a damn bit of difference, does it, when you realize the sacrifice your parents made to get you and Little B Schwinn bikes that had working horns. That was freedom for a kid. Mine even had a basket to carry the papers in. Boy, could I fold them to fit at least fifty or more.

The more you delivered, the more you made. In the big time now. I could go under the viaduct and deliver them in River Forest, Illinois, the big-money town, which is a suburb of Forest Park. Talk about the money places! Even had one house that covered an entire block. A guy named Tony lived there. It was surrounded with a ten-foot-high fence made of wrought iron. I delivered the paper to the cottage his servants lived in. Neither rain, nor sleet, nor hail, nor snow kept me from my appointed rounds. I did it without a government subsidy. Why? In 1945 if you got five dollars from a gangster for Christmas because you put his paper under the awning each time, you did not need a subsidy. You needed an accountant.

The war was over. The tears had dried up, and the world continued on in time to the next war. But there was a big difference this time. The seven-year-old was beginning to realize that he had sometimes forgotten to follow the rules he learned in kindergarten. He thought about that many times, and even one day rode his new bike into the back of a parked car. He and the car and the bike survived. But he thought, "Isn't it about time I took care of myself before going home to Mom?" Who knows, someday I might return and Mom will not be there to take care of me. As he rode his bike home he thought, "How simple it was when I was two. All I had to do then was to receive love. Now I have to learn how to give it also." Sometimes in life you have to learn things the hard way, again and again. But most important is that you learn them, so you can make sure you give love for someone to receive. That is Christmas!

Facing page:
Lucia Nights tower
with trees, Bishop Hill,
by Mike Wendel

"Dancing Elves," by
May Theilgaard Watts

AND
A HAPPY NEW YEAR
FROM – RAYMOND
MAY THEILGAARD
ERICA AND NANCY
WATTS

Sources

INTRODUCTION

Bruce David Forbes. *Christmas: A Candid History.* Berkeley: University of California Press, 2007.

Stephen Nissenbaum. *The Battle for Christmas.* New York: Alfred A. Knopf, 1997.

Donald Culross Peattie. "The Best State of the Fifty." In *Prairie State: Impressions of Illinois, 1673–1967, by Travelers and Other Observers.* Ed. Paul M. Angle. Chicago: University of Chicago Press, 1968. 595–601.

CHRISTMAS IN ILLINOIS HISTORY

Virginia Eifert. "Christmas at Kaskaskia." *Living Museum* 13.8 (December 1951): 246, 248. Reprinted by permission of the Illinois State Museum.

John W. Allen. "Christmas on the Cache." In *Legends and Lore of Southern Illinois.* Carbondale: Area Services, Southern Illinois University, 1963. 225–27. Reprinted by permission of Special Collections Research Center, Morris Library, Southern Illinois University Carbondale.

R. O. White. "Skins as a Circulating Medium." In *History of Bond and Montgomery Counties, Illinois*. Ed. William Henry Perrin. Chicago: O.L. Baskin and Co., 1882. 19. Copy in Bond County Historical Society, Greenville. Courtesy of Linda Hanabarger.

Linda Hanabarger. "Luster Family Has Many Tales to Tell." *Vandalia (Ill.) Leader-Union*, September 4, 2008. Courtesy of the author and the *Vandalia Leader-Union*.

Joseph Smith. *An American Prophet's Record: The Diaries and Journals of Joseph Smith*. Ed. Scott H. Faulring. Salt Lake City: Signature Books in association with Smith Research Associates, 1989. 435. Reprinted by permission of Signature Books.

Presley G. Donaldson. "A Christmas Spree." In *Life and Adventures of P. G. Donaldson*. Cowden, Ill.: Jewett Printery, 1908; reprint, Windmill Publications for Bond County Historical Society. 217–19. Courtesy of Linda Hanabarger.

Owen Muelder. "Christmas the Same as Any Other Day." First published in this anthology. Used with permission of the author.

Tara McClelland McAndrew. "Too Much Spirit: Christmas of 1860 Featured Sleigh Accidents, Brawl, Shooting." *(Springfield, Ill.) State Journal-Register*, December 24, 2004. Reprinted by permission of the author and the *State Journal-Register*.

John B. Reid. "Christmas in 1863: A Civil War Soldier's Account." *Greenville Advocate*, December 21, 2000. Reprinted by permission of Kevin Kaegy, Bond County Genealogical Society.

Marcia D. Young. "How Christmas Came to Clover Lawn." First published in this anthology. Used with permission of the author. The Davis family letters quoted here may be found in two separate collections: the David Davis Family papers in the Abraham Lincoln Presidential Library in Springfield, Illinois, and the Samuel Chapman Armstrong Collection in the archives at Williams College, Williamstown, Massachusetts. The quotation from Lizzy Sedgwick of New York to her cousin, Kate Sedgwick of Lenox, Massachusetts, appears in Nissenbaum, *Battle for Christmas*, 164–65.

"A Christmas Eve Fight." *New York Times*, December 26, 1889.

"After Christmas." *Champaign County Gazette*, December 1898. Courtesy of Urbana Free Library/Champaign County Historical Society Archives.

Hilda Satt Polacheck. *I Came a Stranger: The Story of a Hull-House Girl*. Ed. Dena J. Polacheck Epstein. Urbana: University of Illinois Press, 1991. 51–52. Reprinted by permission of Dena J. Polacheck.

Jack McReynolds. "Black Christmas 1951." *Southern Illinoisan*, December 24, 2006. Reprinted by permission of the author and the *Southern Illinoisan*.

Eloise Jordan. "Christmas in Chicago." *Book Bulletin of the Chicago Public Library* 37.10 (December 1955): 183–85. Reprinted by permission of the Chicago Public Library. Jordan's account of the Christmas Tree Ship is based on a history written by Harry Hansen, literary editor of the *Chicago Daily News.*

LIVING TRADITIONS

"Dear Santa." *Heritage of Vermilion County (Ill.)* 17.1 (Winter 1980–81): 2. Reprinted by permission of the Vermilion County Museum Society.

Robert Green Ingersoll. "What I Want for Christmas." *The Arena* (Boston), December 1897.

John W. Allen. "An Echo of Old Christmas." In *It Happened in Southern Illinois.* Carbondale: Area Services, Southern Illinois University, 1968. 239–41. Reprinted by permission of Special Collections Research Center, Morris Library, Southern Illinois University Carbondale.

"'Jul-otta' Services Here to Draw Ten Thousand Worshipers." *Rockford (Ill.) Morning Star,* December 17, 1950. *Rockford Register Star*/Copyrighted/Used with permission.

Brian Kleeman. "Santa Parade Is Now One Hundred." *Peoria (Ill.) Journal Star,* November 15, 1987. Reprinted by permission of the *Peoria Journal Star.*

Robert Charles Howard. "Belleville Celebrates Its Christmas Traditions." First published in this anthology. Used with permission of the author.

Timothy M. Kovalcik. "Millikin's Gift: The Story of Vespers." First published in this anthology. Used with permission of the author.

Kai Swanson. "Augustana Christmas Traditions." First published in this anthology. Used with permission of the author.

"Youngsters Learn Polish Christmas Custom." *Rockford (Ill.) Observer,* December 8, 1989. Used with permission of the *Observer,* the official newspaper of the Catholic Diocese of Rockford.

Gwendolyn Brooks. "Tradition and Maud Martha." In *Maud Martha.* New York: Harper and Row, 1953. 102–5. Reprinted by consent of Brooks Permissions.

Sandra Cisneros. "Un Poquito de Tu Amor." In *A Family Christmas.* Ed. Caroline Kennedy. New York: Hyperion, 2007. 127–31. Copyright 1998 by Sandra Cisneros. First published in the *Los Angeles Times,* February 1998. Reprinted by permission of Susan Bergholz Literary Services, New York and Lamy, N.M.. All rights reserved.

SONGS AND SYMBOLS

John W. Allen. "Christmas Trees." In *It Happened in Southern Illinois.* Carbondale: Area Services, Southern Illinois University, 1968. 241–42. Reprinted by permission of Special Collections Research Center, Morris Library, Southern Illinois University Carbondale.

The articles in "Songs of Good Cheer" were published as follows: Mary Schmich, "Hark!

Why Isn't Anyone Singing Christmas Carols?" *Chicago Tribune*, December 23, 1998; Eric Zorn, "Jingle Belle Gets a Challenge from O Holy Knight," *Chicago Tribune*, October 17, 1999; Eric Zorn, "'Cheer' Report," *Chicago Tribune*, December 11, 2006. Reprinted with the blessing of the authors and with permission of the *Chicago Tribune*. Copyright Chicago Tribune; all rights reserved.

Theodore Klinka. "Christmas Music in an Illinois Public School." First published in this anthology. Used with permission of the author.

LaDonna Harrell Martin. "Belinda Grey and the Christmas Carol." *Springhouse* 16.6 (December 1999): 43–44. Reprinted by permission of *Springhouse* publishers Gary and Judy DeNeal, Herod, Illinois.

Robert J. Hastings. "A String of Lights for Christmas." Originally published in *A Nickel's Worth of Skimmed Milk: A Boy's View of the Great Depression*. Carbondale: University Graphics and Publications, Southern Illinois University, 1972. 50–55. Copyright © 1972 by the Board of Trustees, Southern Illinois University. Reprinted by permission of the publisher.

"Rockford's First Christmas Tree." *Rockford (Ill.) Morning Star*, December 24, 1911.

John Knoepfle. "Some Words for the Lighting of the Christmas Tree in the Auburn, Illinois, Town Square." In *The Chinkapin Oak*. Springfield, Ill.: Rose Hill Press, 1995. 69–70. Used with permission of the author.

CHRISTMAS OUTDOORS

Joel Greenberg. "Holidays with Feathers: Forty Years of Christmas Bird Counts." First published in this anthology. Used with permission of the author.

Ben Gelman. "December 25, 1983." Originally published in *Bird Watching with Ben*. Carbondale: Southern Illinois University Press, 1985. 143–45. Copyright © 1985 by the Board of Trustees, Southern Illinois University. Reprinted by permission of the publisher.

Carl Sandburg. "Star Silver." In *Sandburg Range*. New York: Harcourt, Brace, and Co., 1957. Copyright 1957 by Carl Sandburg and renewed 1985 by Margaret Sandburg, Janet Sandburg, and Helga Sandburg Crile. Reprinted by permission of Houghton Mifflin Harcourt Publishing Company.

May Theilgaard Watts. "They Wear the Snow with a Difference." *Morton Arboretum Bulletin of Popular Information* 20.1 (January 1945): 1–4. Courtesy of the Sterling Morton Library, the Morton Arboretum, Lisle, Illlinois.

Dixie Terry. "From My Kitchen Window, Christmas 1999." *Springhouse* 16.6 (December 1999): 23–26. Used with permission of the author and *Springhouse* publishers Gary and Judy DeNeal, Herod, Illinois.

Laura H. Holman. "Old Time Recipes," *Outdoor Illinois* 9.10 (December 1970): 32. Used with permission of Laura Holman's granddaughters, Vickee Cockrum and Judy Eubanks.

Elisabeth S. Carus. "Stuffing, Cookies, and Klaben." Copyright 2004 by Elisabeth S. Carus. Used with permission of the author.

Hermilda Listeman. "Collinsville's Queen of Cookies." First published in this anthology. Courtesy of May Berenbaum and Richard and Hannah Leskosky.

Marjorie Abrath Snyder. "Noisy Cookies and Pickled Smelt/Herring." First published in this anthology. Used with permission of the author.

Dean Yannias. "Christmas Dinner without End, Amen." First published in this anthology. Used with permission of the author.

Edna Michael. "Christmas in the Early 1900s." *Heritage of Vermilion County (Ill.)* 18.1 (Winter 1981–82): 12, 18. Reprinted by permission of the Vermilion County Museum Society.

Carolyn Neal. "Childhood Memories." First published in this anthology. Used with permission of the author.

Virginia Long. "Oranges." First published in this anthology. Used with permission of the author.

Ron Hornberger. "Christmas Comes Early for Thatch." *Cairo (Ill.) Citizen*, December 12, 1984. Reprinted by permission of the *Cairo Citizen*.

Edgar Allen Imhoff. "The Christmas Fox." Originally published in *Always of Home: A Southern Illinois Childhood*. Carbondale: Southern Illinois University Press, 1993. 10–11. Copyright © 1993 by the Board of Trustees, Southern Illinois University. Reprinted by permission of the publisher.

Fred Butler. "The Cannon House at Christmas." *Heritage of Vermilion County (Ill.).* 18.1 (Winter 1981–82): 4. Reprinted by permission of the Vermilion County Museum Society.

Andrew Durdan. "Diary of a Farmer on Christmas, 1945." From *1945 Andrew Durdan Farm: One Year in the Life of an Illinois Farming Family*. Ed. Jeff Sparks and Esther Durdan Sparks. Naples, Fla.: Privately printed, 2007. 206–17. Adapted for this anthology and used with permission of Jeff Sparks.

Ruth Hanna Noble. "Holiday Memories." First published in this anthology. Used with the permission of her daughter, Priscilla Grundy.

Marie Rose Ellis. "Christmas in Naperville." Composed in the late 1920s and first published in this anthology. Used with permission of the Naper Settlement archives in Naperville and with the kind courtesy of Evelyn Hankel and Eileen Burton.

Sarah Bunting. "Christmas Comes." *Heritage of Vermilion County (Ill.)*. 16.1 (Winter 1979–80): 4. Reprinted by permission of the Vermilion County Museum Society.

Jim May. "Christmas Eve in the Barn." In *The Farm on Nippersink Creek*. Little Rock: August House, 1994. 39–55. Adapted for this anthology and used with permission of the author.

Mary Miritello. "My Grandfather's Treasure." First published in this anthology. Used with permission of the author.

Channy Lyons. "Mother and Daughter, Christmas Eve." First published in this anthology. Used with permission of the author.

Violet Trovillion and Hal W. Trovillion. *Christmas at Thatchcot*. Booklet. Herrin, Ill.: Trovillion Private Press, 1947. Courtesy of the Herrin Public Library.

Mike Royko. "Mary and Joe Chicago-Style." *Chicago Daily News*, December 19, 1967. Courtesy of *Chicago Daily News*.

Richard Klemp. "That Is Christmas." First published in this anthology. Used with permission of the author.

ILLUSTRATIONS

p. ii   Christmas tree, by May Theilgaard Watts. Courtesy of the heirs of May Theilgaard Watts.

p. 14   Bringing in the Yule Log at the Morton Arboretum. Photograph by Jim Nachel. Courtesy of the Sterling Morton Library, the Morton Arboretum.

p. 22   David Davis Mansion at Christmas. Photograph by Dave Wilson. Courtesy of the David Davis Mansion, a state historical site.

p. 29   J. P. McCollum home, Champaign, 1950. Curt Breamer, photographer. Reproduced by permission of The News-Gazette, Inc. Permission does not imply endorsement.

p. 33   Cover drawing by Robert Youngman for *Our Christmas Disaster*, 1952, a booklet written by C. Edwin Hair, former mayor of Benton. Courtesy of Robert Rea, the Franklin County Jail Museum, and the Franklin County Historic Preservation Society.

p. 36   State Street in Christmas dress, 1941. Provenance of State Street Council. Used by permission of Chicago Public Library, Special Collections and Preservation Division, CLAC o/s 2/6.

p. 37   Cratchets' Christmas Dinner, Slotkowski Sausage Co. float, 1968. Used by permission of Chicago Public Library, Special Collections and Preservation Division, CLAC 6/4 (12).

p. 37   Angels on float in front of the Chicago Theater, 1956. Used by permission of Chicago Public Library, Special Collections and Preservation Division, CLAC 4/4 (13).

p. 40 Greetings from Thornhill, the Morton Arboretum, 1931. Courtesy of the Sterling Morton Archives.

p. 42 Julbock and Tomten. Courtesy of Mike Wendel, photographer, and the Bishop Hill Heritage Association.

p. 44 Santa's letter box, 1958. Used with permission of Chicago Public Library, Special Collections and Preservation Division, CLAC 4/4 (1). Image by Pics Chicago. The photograph is of Susie Heinkel, the Chicago teenage star of CBS-TV's *Susan's Show*, as she drops the first letter in one of sixteen boxes along State Street. All letters were answered with a gift of a lollipop or balloon.

p. 51 "A Christmas Message," crossword puzzle by Art Geisert. Courtesy of Art Geisert.

p. 55 Santa Lucias, Bishop Hill. Courtesy of Mike Wendel, photographer, and the Bishop Hill Heritage Association.

p. 57 Santa Claus Headquarters, Peoria. Image courtesy R. W. Deller Collection and Peoria Historical Society Collection, Bradley University Library.

p. 57 Caterpillar and Mother Goose, Peoria. Image courtesy R. W. Deller Collection and Peoria Historical Society Collection, Bradley University Library.

p. 58 Santa Parade, Main Street, Peoria. Image courtesy R. W. Deller Collection and Peoria Historical Society Collection, Bradley University Library.

p. 62 Trolley in the Square, Belleville. Courtesy Belleville Chamber of Commerce.

p. 62 Santa Claus House, Belleville. Courtesy Belleville Chamber of Commerce.

p. 66 Millikin Vespers tableau, 1932. Courtesy Millikin University Archives and Special Collections and the *Decatur Herald and Review*.

p. 66 Millikin Vespers, 1992. Courtesy Millikin University Archives and Special Collections.

p. 80 Christmas 1915, Peoria County. Photographer unknown. Courtesy of Bradley University Special Collections.

p. 82 Christmas 1900, Union County. Photographer unknown. From the collection of Judy Travelstead, Cobden.

p. 84 University of Illinois Madrigal Singers, 1969. Courtesy of the University of Illinois Archives.

p. 90 Studs Terkel, Songs of Good Cheer, Old Town School of Music, 2006. Used with permission of the photographer, Steve Kagan.

p. 90 Hessel Park Reformed Church, Champaign. Courtesy of the Champaign County Historical Archives, The Urbana Free Library, Urbana, Ill.

p. 93 New Trier Chorus and Orchestra, 1953. Courtesy of New Trier High School.

p. 96 Christmas tree drawing by May Theilgaard Watts. Courtesy of the heirs of May Theilgaard Watts.

p. 100 Drawing of the Jo Daviess County post office, by Art Geisert. Courtesy of Art Geisert.

p. 105 "Santa Marching to Work, 1895," by Edgar Rice Burroughs. Used with permission of Bill Hillman, editor and Webmaster for the Edgar Rice Burroughs Websites and

Webzines, http://www.erbzine.com/xmas. From the Michigan Military Academy's *Christmas Adjutant*, of which Burroughs, a Chicago resident, was an editor.

p. 106   Snow Road, Saline County. Courtesy of Charles Hammond, photographer.

p. 108   Snowy cardinal, Galena. Copyright Barbara Baird. Courtesy of the photographer.

p. 113   "Christmas Morning on the Illinois River," by David Zalaznik. Used with permission of the photographer, from his book *Life along the Illinois River* (Urbana: University of Illinois Press, 2008).

p. 116   "December Snow on the Branches," by May Theilgaard Watts, 1945. Courtesy of the heirs of May Theilgaard Watts.

p. 118   "Some Ways of Wearing the Snow," by May Theilgaard Watts. *Morton Arboretum Bulletin of Popular Information* 20.1 (January 1945): 3. Courtesy of the Sterling Morton Library, the Morton Arboretum.

p. 121   "Treed by a Moose," by Edgar Rice Burroughs. Family Christmas card, ca. 1909. Used with permission of Bill Hillman, editor and Webmaster for the Edgar Rice Burroughs Websites and Webzines, http://www.erbzine.com/xmas.

p. 122   Emily Droege of Galva as a Lucia. Courtesy of Mike Wendel, photographer, and the Bishop Hill Heritage Association.

p. 124   Table set for Christmas dinner at the David Davis Mansion. Photograph by Ken Kashian. Courtesy of the David Davis Mansion, a state historical site.

p. 147   "A Guide to Citizens," by Art Geisert. Courtesy of Art Geisert.

p. 150   Lincoln and Douglas dressed for Christmas in Washington Park, Ottawa. Courtesy of James Ballowe.

p. 161   The Cannon House at Christmas, ca. 1920s. From the photo archives of the Vermilion County Museum Society.

p. 169   Marie Rose Ellis at the Germann Home, ca. 1920. Courtesy of Evelyn Hankel and Eileen Burton.

p. 181   Saverio Fratto's *presepio* Nativity scene, 1945. Courtesy of Mary Miritello.

p. 190   "Dancing Elves," by May Theilgaard Watts. Courtesy of the heirs of May Theilgaard Watts.

p. 191   Lucia Nights tower with tree, Bishop Hill. Courtesy of Mike Wendel, photographer, and the Bishop Hill Heritage Association.

A native of Herrin, **JAMES BALLOWE** is a Distinguished Professor Emeritus
of English at Bradley University. He is the author of, most recently, *A Man of
Salt and Trees: The Life of Joy Morton*. He lives in Ottawa, Illinois.
Author photo by Ruth Ganchiff.

The University of Illinois Press is a founding member
of the Association of American University Presses.

Designed by Copenhaver Cumpston

Composed in 11/14 Adobe Jenson Pro, an Adobe original
designed by Robert Slimbach. Adobe Jenson Pro is a historical
revival of the work of Nicholas Jenson (c. 1420–1480),
a Venetian printer and type designer.
It captures the essence of Nicolas Jenson's roman
and Ludovico degli Arrighi's italic typeface designs, with
the wide library of specialized characters available
in the open type format.

Typeset by Jim Proefrock at the University of Illinois Press

Manufactured by Sheridan Books, Inc.

UNIVERSITY OF ILLINOIS PRESS
1325 South Oak Street   Champaign, IL 61820-6903
www.press.uillinois.edu